Retirement Your Way
Online Course

Thank you for reading *Retirement Your Way!*

We invite you to continue your journey into your
Next Chapter by visiting our website at
www.RetirementYourWayBook.com
where you will find more information about our offerings,
including coaching, speaking, and...

Our online video course designed to enhance the ideas
offered in this book. When you enroll in the online course,
you'll get a comprehensive guidebook, plus lifetime access
to a series of short, online videos that you can watch at your
own pace, anywhere, and on any device.

A short, fun quiz to help you see possibilities for thriving
in your Next Chapter. The quiz is based on the six lifestyle
categories introduced in Conversations One and Three.

Enjoy the journey as you let go of your stories,
add your dreams, and keep exploring!

Marilyn and Gail

ENDORSEMENTS

"One of a kind. *Retirement Your Way* offers a simple, innovative path to living a life of contribution and self-fulfillment. If you are approaching retirement, this is a must read."

— **Marshall Goldsmith,** *New York Times* #1 Bestselling Author of *Triggers, Mojo,* and *What Got You Here Won't Get You There*

"Imaginative and inspiring! The definitive roadmap for navigating the uncertain and often emotional journey of retirement."

— **Noah Blumenthal,** Bestselling Author of *Be the Hero: Three Powerful Ways to Overcome Challenges in Work and Life*

"Practical, profound and fun to read, *Retirement Your Way* is the book for you if you are even beginning to think about retirement. The CHOICES Map is helping me to think through and plan my transition into my Next Chapter, and it sparked my imagination about what is possible now and in the future. I am proud to say that I'm officially in phase 1 of my 'stair stepper' plan. This book will definitely be a go-to reference as I design the next stages of my life. It's an exciting time and having *Retirement Your Way* is just what I needed."

— **Lisa Rickard,** President of the U.S. Chamber Institute for Legal Reform

"People would not marry a new spouse without some serious dating and courtship, and they would not start up a new job without checking out the company, its products, and the expectations others have for them. Yet many people jump into retirement without even thinking through the implications.

When my father retired, I asked him what he was going to do and he replied, "Go fishing." The first week he went fishing five days, the next week three days, the third week one day, and then he never went fishing again. I asked him why, and he said, 'It's more fun thinking about it than actually doing it.'

This book not only provides valuable information and insights on retirement, but it is also designed to help you ask yourself the critical questions necessary for you to find joy in your next chapter. A must read for everyone, whether you are retiring this year or not planning to retire but are looking at a change."

— **Joseph Folkman,** President, Zenger Folkman, and Co-author of *How to Be Exceptional: Drive Leadership Success by Magnifying Your Strengths* and *The Extraordinary Leader: Turning Good Managers into Great Leaders*

"Enjoy your guided journey into your next chapter through Gail and Marilyn's CHOICES Map highlighting the 7 essential conversations to help you re-envision and design your retirement. This fresh and insightful look at the next phase in career and life will prompt you to explore old assumptions and choose what you want for your future rather than drift along without insight or choice. The authors have done an amazing job uncovering the outdated and, for many, the undesirable story of what retirement looks like to offer a new paradigm. This powerful book is an essential read for anyone approaching or already in this next phase of life. Through humor, quotes, and storytelling, you will find yourself eager to engage with their reflective questions and begin to design your Next Chapter!"

— **Amy Vodarek,** Amy Vodarek and Associates, Co-author of *Good Enough. Embrace Who You Are. Unleash Your Brilliance*

"As someone who is in the pre-retirement years, most of the guidance and advice I have been given on the topic has centered around whether my financial plan is adequate. It is so refreshing to find a book with sage and thoughtful advice on who I want to be and *can* be in retirement! Marilyn and Gail's focus on the human side has me more excited and grounded about this topic than I've ever been! And while I'm not rushing to get there, I feel that there's a world of new possibilities awaiting me once my journey arrives!"

— **Mike Jaffe,** The Human WakeUp Call®, Founder, the Mike Jaffe Company and Author of *Wake Up! Your Life Is Calling*

"*Retirement Your Way* is a much needed new conversation addressing the 'retirement' story that has been so much a part of our recent generations. It's about time we see our Next Chapter as a rich time of active accomplishment, relevant contribution, and an opportunity to share a lifetime of wisdom with others. This can be our harvest season for a lifetime of learning and experience — a time when we focus on our deepest passions and make our most meaningful contributions.

I have always wanted to live my later years as a time of freedom and rich meaning, not a barren stretch of isolation, empty time, and money worries. I'm now in my seventies and discovering firsthand that the elder years can be a time of greater freedom and choice — if only we are able to live in stories that enable us to see our choices, make preparations, and get to know our hearts and souls better.

Retirement Your Way provides these new perspectives, along with practical guidance for facing the Next Chapter. It shows how we can take this opportunity to realize our dreams and create our lives as our own work of art with deep satisfaction, connection, joy, and relevance. This is the journey worth taking."

— **Bob Dunham,** Founder of the Institute for Generative
Leadership and Co-author of *The Innovator's Way*

"Our culture provides more guidance for selecting a kitchen blender than for designing the later third of your life. Here's the missing manual. There's no 'right way' to work, and this book shows there are as many options for the Next Chapter after work. This book lays out the questions and possibilities so clearly and beautifully. Through the questions and real examples the authors share, readers will see fresh ideas and be able to design an approach that suits their values, circumstances, and the calling of their hearts."

— **Pam Fox Rollin,** Executive Coach and Author
of *42 Rules for Your New Leadership Role*

RETIREMENT
YOUR
WAY

RETIREMENT YOUR WAY

The **No Stress** Roadmap for Designing
Your Next Chapter and Loving Your Future

Gail M. McDonald **&** Marilyn L. Bushey

CHOICES
NEXT

First published by Choices Next LLC

Copyright © 2019 by Choices Next LLC

First Edition

Choices Next LLC

P.O. Box 477

Lake Dallas, TX 75065

info@retirementyourwaybook.com

www.retirementyourwaybook.com

Library of Congress Control Number: 2018967635

978-1-7336874-0-9 (paperback)

978-1-7336874-1-6 (ebook)

We dedicate this book to our husbands, Jeff and Brian. As retirees, you are Traditionalists. As men, you follow your own paths. As life partners, you are our constant supporters, our cheerleaders, and our best friends. Words can't express our love and gratitude to you for being in our lives.

Table of Contents

APPENDICES

The Journey Begins

"**W**hat does retirement mean to you?"

That was the supposedly simple question we asked during a conversation with a good friend, *Valerie Fulbright*. Her reaction, especially the emotion associated with it, surprised us.

She snapped back, "I hadn't thought about retirement. Retirement means *quit* to me. I'm not quitting anything . . . I don't feel like I've finished doing what I do best."

Valerie reacted to the word *retirement* emphatically. Although we hadn't expected such an emotional response, once we heard it, it resonated with us. We felt our own sense of rebellion against the traditional concept of retirement and suspected that we and Valerie were not alone. Many of our peers who were approaching or had even passed the traditional age of retirement were full of energy, had a zest for life, and enjoyed their careers. If they were anything like us, they were probably thinking, "Why stop now?"

As Valerie put it, "I enjoy what I do. It's hard to let go of what you enjoy." We would add, why should any of us need to stop doing what we enjoy anyway? Why do people need to give up work just because they hit a certain age?

Even those who want to retire from their jobs are not necessarily ready to withdraw from the work world altogether. They are looking at their next steps with wonder and interest. They know they want to stay engaged, to create, to contribute, and to leave a legacy. They are not ready to be put out to pasture by a Western society that overvalues youth and often disregards the wisdom and beauty of people beyond a certain age.

As *Financial Advisor* author Richard Wagner put it, "'Retired' just does not work for this time. It not only is imprecise, it deflates. It was for our grandparents, not us. And it just keeps on meaning 'tired.'"[1]

NOT YOUR PARENTS' RETIREMENT

Many of us have a sense that we want to navigate this territory in a different way than our predecessors. We personally agree with Wagner, and clearly our friend Valerie did, too. With Valerie's intense reaction, we realized that perhaps it's time to reinvent retirement, and the idea for this book was born.

On the basis of conversations with Valerie and others, we began our exploration of retirement—and its alternatives. We interviewed numerous friends, colleagues, and acquaintances who were retired, who could retire whenever they wanted, or who were considering retirement within the next five to ten years. We wanted to understand what they were thinking, feeling, and experiencing during this time of their lives. Also, we wanted to inspire ourselves and others to live with gusto and optimism.

The more we talked to our contemporaries, the more fascinated we became, partly because of the growing number of baby boomers who had reached or were approaching retirement age—and partly because we were struggling with decisions around retirement ourselves.

One of the first things we learned was that many of us have an aversion to the word *retirement*. We had heard this from Valerie. We shared it ourselves, and we heard it again and again from others.

As a result, we use the term *Next Chapter* interchangeably with the word *retirement* to reflect this time of life, which begins typically in our mid-60s and occurs after what is generally thought of as "traditional work." One of the reasons we like the term *Next Chapter* is because it applies to all people who reach a certain stage of life, regardless of whether their work involves a paycheck or not.

Also, people can have multiple Next Chapters, whereas the term *Third Act* (which we also considered for use in this book)—or even, to some extent, *Third Chapter*—signals a sense of finality. We believe that the Next Chapter may have more than one phase, and we want to encourage you to value each phase that you experience.

During our conversations with our contemporaries, we also learned that many people base their retirement decisions first on financial or health considerations. This makes sense. There are times in everyone's life when they must focus on those areas. We also realize that many experts provide superb advice targeted at helping individuals and families navigate important financial or health decisions. That is not our area of expertise.

In this book, we focus on the opportunities and choices that people have when they are able to look beyond financial and health priorities or when they simply want to take a break from these concerns long enough to consider and dream about their ideal future lifestyles.

As we continued our informal research and conversations, we noticed that our contemporaries were intrigued and even excited about what we were asking. They wanted to learn more about our research and the model that we were developing.

The more conversations we had with other people and with each other, the more convinced we became that we had something of value to explore and share. And so we began the journey of writing this book.

This book is about questioning the assumptions that you hold about retirement and expanding the possibilities that you envision. Fundamentally, we are celebrating a retirement revolution. We applaud all of you who do not automatically accept the tried and true. You are inventing new ways of contributing to society, having fun, and living fully. You are the new Retirement Rebels.

THE IMPORTANCE OF CHOICE

As we continued our conversations and research, we began to notice similarities among people's stories and see patterns emerging from our research. From these patterns, we synthesized three primary themes that form the foundation of this book.

The first theme is that retirement calls for one thing—choice! Most of us have many more lifestyle choices than we might have expected.

The second theme is that these choices often boil down to three types of decisions: What we let go, what we add, and what we keep in our lives. From this realization, we developed our mantra for the book.

> **Let go of your stories**
> **Add your dreams**
> **Keep exploring**

The third theme is that the Next Chapter is a more emotional time than most of us expect. Although many individuals have moved through this stage of life before us, the territory may at times feel rocky, uncertain, and largely unknown.

Given that most people have many choices and that there is frequently an emotional component underlying these choices, we believe that there is a need for a practical roadmap to guide individuals through the new territory.

As a result, to help you navigate the twists and turns of this often emotional journey, we created the CHOICES Map. It is a roadmap to help you make decisions about what to let go, what to add, and what to keep as you enter this Next Chapter of your life.

The CHOICES Map is a practical approach to guide you as you leave behind the stories that hold you back, as you incorporate your dreams and passions into your Next Chapter, and as you continue to explore and learn throughout your life. Our intention is that this approach will help guide you into your healthiest and happiest version of retirement—or nonretirement, whichever the case may be.

We introduce the CHOICES Map in the next chapter and explore each of its components in the following chapters.

NAVIGATING THE BOOK

In this book, we use the metaphor of a journey to explore the concerns, priorities, questions, and decisions that many of us encounter during the Next Chapter. We think of ourselves and our contemporaries as Retirement Rebels—people who are looking for a new path to our future.

Our belief is that all people have the answers within them for living their best lives. Each of us makes a different decision regarding the best path at any specific moment in time. We hope that the examples from other people featured in this book and the CHOICES Map we have created will help you become even clearer about your own truth so that you can design the Next Chapter you truly desire.

We have included some special features and tools to assist you on your journey into your Next Chapter. We hope that they make your journey more enjoyable and gratifying.

Songs

In some chapters we chose to refer to music that was popular when baby boomers were growing up. Our aspiration is that you will identify with these songs and that they will bring back memories and dreams. Maybe you will even find yourself humming some of these songs as you go through the day, and they will guide your thoughts back to the book and bring a smile to your face.

Quotes, Stories, and Examples

We have also inserted many quotes, stories, and examples, including our own, to encourage you to reflect on your own experiences, become aware of new possibilities for the future, and create a personal roadmap for what can be the most satisfying and exciting time of your life. Have fun reading about how other people are navigating their Next Chapter, and let them become your imaginary conversation partners as you move through the book. We are all in this together!

Conversation Starters

As you will discover, we chose the concept of conversations as our vehicle to traverse the CHOICES Map. Conversations help people to see their choices and to select the best path going forward. As you read this book and design your Next Chapter, you may have conversations with yourself, with others, and with the broader universe. In each chapter, we have included two or three questions to help you think about the impact of the chapter on your own life and to kick-start the conversations that may be helpful to you.

Rest Stops

At the end of each chapter, we've included a special section called Rest Stop. The purpose of the Rest Stop is to help you pause and reflect beyond the direct content of the chapter before you move on to the next conversation.

Navigating Your Way

Depending on your purpose, you have many options for how to approach this book. If you would like to use this book as a guide to help you design your next stage of life, we suggest that you read each chapter in order and work through the exercises and conversation starters. You could do this by yourself, with your spouse, or with a coach.

Perhaps you might even want to read the book with some friends or your book club and serve as peer coaches for one another. As you read this book, you might consider getting a special notebook or journal, where you can write your answers to the exercises or doodle about what inspires you. This will help you stay organized, take real action, and have a personalized reference aid.

Alternatively, if you want to touch on this topic more lightly, then you might want to read or skim the book without doing the exercises. If you are interested in a specific topic, you might want to go directly to the chapter that addresses it.

Since your life circumstances will change as you move through the upcoming years, it is inevitable that you will revisit decisions that you made previously. There are hundreds of reasons that might lead you to reevaluate your earlier choices and identify new actions that you want to take. At these times, we suggest that you pick up the book and revisit the CHOICES Map.

CALLING ALL RETIREMENT REBELS

Our primary aspiration in writing this book is to help you find meaning, contribution, and fulfillment in your Next Chapter. We firmly believe that most people have the talent, energy, and drive needed to contribute to the world well beyond their traditional retirement years.

Our goal for this book is that it will serve as a bridge to a bigger and more fulfilling life than you ever imagined. We hope that the messages within each chapter encourage you to be a confident explorer and to trust yourself as you navigate this journey. In doing so, you will undoubtedly choose the paths that energize you, bring you alive, and connect you to your purpose on this planet.

Along the way, we hope that you, the reader, experience some *aha* moments, have some good laughs, see new possibilities for your own journey, and help to reboot our cultural view of retirement!

Every personal story has the potential to inspire others. We'd love to hear how your journey into your Next Chapter is going. Please visit our website (www.retirementyourwaybook.com) to see our latest offerings or our Facebook page (Retirement Your Way) to join the conversation and share your story with others.

We dedicate this book to a new group of rebels: those who are navigating retirement—and all its alternatives—in a different way. You are forging new paths and opening up new possibilities for yourselves and those who follow you.

Let the journey begin!

—Marilyn and Gail

A Roadmap for Your Next Chapter

Where do I go from here? This is a question many of us ask as we approach retirement or when we realize that our current retirement is not what we had imagined.

For many of us, retirement, or the Next Chapter, represents a big unknown. It's exciting—a time to do what we want, a time of freedom. Yet it can also be overwhelming. It's a time when we must come up with our own answers and make choices about how we structure our days, how we continue to contribute value to society, how we stay fulfilled as human beings, and how we live out our life purposes.

Often, we don't know these answers. We might look at our options as being limited, whereas the truth is that we have many more choices than we might realize.

The word *choices* represents a key theme of this book. Why? At this point in our lives, most of us are discovering that we have an array of rich, vibrant options for our Next Chapter; in fact, we all have many more choices than we might have previously envisioned. If you don't yet see your choices, we hope that this book will go a long way to helping you discover them.

In addition to being a central theme of this book, the word *CHOICES* is an acronym for seven critical conversations that we believe are essential components for navigating your journey into a new stage of life.

The seven conversations are designed to help guide and energize you as you enter new, often murky territory. These seven conversations make up the CHOICES Map.

In this book, conversations are our vehicle to traverse the CHOICES Map. We use the word *conversation* in two ways. First, we refer to "7 Conversations," each of which represents an important step of the CHOICES Map. In this context, we use the term broadly—somewhat symbolically—to represent the multifaceted, fluid engagement that is possible within each chapter.

As you engage with the content of each chapter, you are likely to have several more tangible conversations. Some of these conversations will be with yourself, some with others, and some with the broader universe. Additionally, these conversations can take place mentally, verbally, nonverbally, or in writing.

Although the conversations are presented as if they are distinct and sequential, they are, in fact, highly interconnected and not perfectly sequential. As you move through your own journey, keep in mind that you may find yourself repeating portions of earlier stages, typically with a deeper level of insight and understanding.

EXPLORING CONVERSATIONS

What do we mean when we say *conversations*? Conversations can be with yourself, with others, or with the broader universe. Most frequently, we think of conversations as an exchange of thoughts, feelings, or ideas between two or more people, ideally on behalf of a shared purpose. Conversations are taking place all around us. Effective conversations are fluid, rich, and engaging, and they have the power to generate action.

There are many types of conversations, and often these

different types intermingle as part of one larger interaction. For example, there are relatively simple conversations to share or to ask for information. There are strategic conversations about possibilities and opportunities to create a shared future. There are conversations focused on brainstorming and innovation. There are conversations with a purpose to coordinate action across two or more people. There are problem-solving conversations to resolve issues and to manage breakdowns. There are conversations to make requests, offers, and promises or commitments.

There are also conversations to share deep concerns, personal emotions, and moods. Sometimes conversations build trust, and sometimes they reduce trust. Clearly, the goal of this book is to build trust as you have conversations regarding your Next Chapter! Whether you are gathering information or enlisting someone's support, trust is essential.

There are conversations that give you a chance to declare your vision for the Next Chapter out loud. A declaration is defined as "speaking that brings something into existence."[1] Declarations are one of six fundamental speech acts that can be described as generative, meaning that the speech acts bring about action and outcomes. The other speech acts include requests, promises, offers, assessments (opinions), and assertions (facts).*

Fernando Flores, a writer and teacher about the role of conversations, said, "People don't merely use language to communicate their desires about the future; they create the future in language together by making commitments to each other. Conversation, then, is not merely a prelude to action; it is its very essence."[2]

---

* This body of work initially evolved from John Austin, a philosopher at Oxford University who distinguished language that is descriptive from language that has the power to generate action. It was further developed and refined by John Searle, Fernando Flores, Julio Olalla, Bob Dunham, and many others.

> We invite you to join us in a conversation to create your desired future and bring your vision for your Next Chapter to life!

THE CHOICES MAP

These are the 7 conversations that make up the CHOICES Map, along with a brief description of each one.

 Conversation 1—Culture: Check Your Rearview Mirror: Recognizing the Impact of Cultural Norms and Practices

This conversation provides a brief history of retirement and how it has changed over time, particularly in the United States and other Western countries. Its purpose is to help you become aware of the cultural norms and beliefs about retirement that you might have been exposed to in your childhood and early adulthood.

Conversation 2—Hurdles: Watch Out for Speed Bumps: Noticing Your Personal Beliefs and Stories That Help or Hinder You

This conversation is about recognizing the beliefs and stories that you have internalized, whether they come from your upbringing or whether you have somehow adopted them as a result of your life experiences. Some of these beliefs help you, whereas others represent significant hurdles. Either way, the key is to become aware of your own beliefs and to let go of the ones that do not serve you anymore.

 Conversation 3—Options: Choose Your Route: Stepping Up to Your Personal Power and Making a Choice

This conversation is your choice point. In fact, it is more than a choice point; it is the time when you fully commit to how you want to navigate the Next Chapter of your life or, more accurately, at least your next steps within the Next Chapter. This conversation also introduces six broad categories, including actual, real-life examples, that describe different lifestyle choices. These are designed to stimulate possibilities beyond what you might have already been considering.

 Conversation 4—Inspiration: Select Your Traveling Companions: Opening Your Heart and Connecting With Your Supporters

This conversation primarily engages your heart as you begin to act on the choices you made in Conversation 3. Here, you intentionally draw into your world whatever inspires and motivates you to live your life with meaning and purpose. You also intentionally reach out to the people who energize, support, and constructively challenge you. These people are your team, and they will be your traveling companions on your road trip—metaphorically or actually!

Conversation 5—Course of Action: Put the Pedal to the Metal: Creating a Plan for Your Journey

This conversation primarily engages your head as you continue to take action on the choices you have made. It is a conversation familiar to many people, particularly those who have worked in the business world. Essentially, you are putting a voice to your new goals. Ideally, you will prepare a written action plan, either in a few words or as a more detailed document. This plan then becomes a guide for your next chapter.

Conversation 6—Experimentation: Head Out on the Open Road: Staying Aware and Continuing to Learn

At this point, you have your plan. Now you allow yourself to move beyond that plan. You experiment with various options and discover that some options work, while others don't. While experimenting, you continue to stay aware of and curious about the world around and within you. In many ways, you adopt the mindset of a lifelong learner. You explore, and you allow yourself to evolve as you move through the various phases of your Next Chapter.

Conversation 7—Self-Fulfillment: Find Your Yellow Brick Road: Connecting With Your Higher Purpose and Lightening Up

This is the final conversation, which focuses on your state of being rather than your state of doing. Often, we describe this conversation as connecting to your spirituality. Fundamentally, this is the state in which you recognize your connection to a higher power and to everything and everyone around you. At the same time, you approach your life with an enhanced sense of play, humor, and lightness.

THE MANTRA AND THE 7 CONVERSATIONS

How does our mantra—*let go of your stories, add your dreams, and keep exploring*—relate to the 7 conversations? First, the three types of decisions within the mantra—let go, add, and keep—are woven throughout each conversation, sometimes directly and sometimes indirectly through the exercises. Additionally, each type of decision is particularly prevalent in certain conversations, as explained here.

- **Let go of your stories.** The first two conversations—Culture and Hurdles—provide an opportunity for you to observe the prevalent retirement beliefs and practices in your family and culture of origin. From these observations, you can identify the stories and beliefs that you have adopted and that no longer serve you. These are the stories you will let go.
- **Add your dreams.** The next three conversations—Options, Inspiration, and Course of Action—encourage you to make lifestyle choices—at least for now—and then to initiate action by reaching out to key people and by creating a plan. During these conversations, you will want to contemplate your desires and perhaps recall your childhood dreams, so that your choices and actions are aligned with what you most care about for your Next Chapter.
- **Keep exploring.** The last two conversations—Experimentation and Self-Fulfillment—address how you want to live for the rest of your life. You experiment, learn, laugh, play, and love. Living with a mindset of exploration fosters vitality, aliveness, and joy.

The road ahead is full of many wonderful options, and the CHOICES Map is your essential guide to designing your Next Chapter, with a smile on your face and joy in your heart. As you prepare to make the right next move for you, have fun on the journey. Enjoy the conversations you will be having with yourself, the people you care about, and the larger universe. Be willing to explore, and know that no matter which route you take, your own internal GPS is there to keep you on course to your desired destination.

Culture: Check Your Rearview Mirror

Your old road is rapidly agin'
Please get out of the new one if you can't lend your hand
For the times they are a-changin'
The line it is drawn
The curse it is cast
The slow one now
Will later be fast
As the present now
Will later be past
The order is rapidly fadin'
And the first one now will later be last
For the times they are a-changin'

—BOB DYLAN, "THE TIMES THEY ARE A-CHANGIN'"

CULTURE

Recognizing the Impact of Cultural Norms and Practices

We are all products of cultural and societal norms, whether they come from our profession, our family history, the country we live in, the specific region we are from, our religious background, or another related area. Often, we are affected by these norms and the practices that accompany them without questioning their value or impact in our own lives. Retirement is one of those areas strongly affected by our cultural perspectives.

When it comes to planning retirement, most of us face pressures from our cultures and our families without even realizing it. We see certain norms in the movies, on television, in our families of origin, and in the lives of our friends and their families. People say things to us that convey ideas about what we should be doing at a certain age.

When we're young, most of us don't pay attention to conversations about retirement—when those conversations occur, how they occur, the value of retiring or not, and so on. Although you might not consciously reflect on these norms and expectations, they most likely sink into your psyche and affect your own beliefs about how you should spend your Next Chapter.

When you don't ask yourself what you want your retirement to look like, you might end up accepting the mantle of what society teaches us all over the years, or you might automatically rebel against it.

CULTURAL PORTALS

Work by Dr. Mario Martinez seems to confirm our discussion of the cultural aspects of the Next Chapter. While doing research on centenarians, Dr. Martinez identified his *theory of cultural portals.*[1] According to Dr. Martinez, cultural portals are "culturally defined segments . . . of expected beliefs and conduct." These segments include the newborn, infancy, childhood, adolescence, young adult, middle age, and—no surprise!—old age portals.

The old age portal—and all portals, in fact—has unspoken cultural rules that may lead people to act in certain ways while they are in that portal. We hope you can become more cognizant of these rules as you progress through Conversation 1 so you can make conscious choices about how to respond to them.

Retirement is one of the unspoken cultural rules in the old age portal. In the United States, there are two accepted norms around retirement that people have followed for years. The first is an exact year at which old age begins (for the first baby boomers, that was 65). The second is the belief that government should pay people for growing old—hence Social Security.

The restrictions society has placed around the old age portal due to cultural norms include the following:

- Many companies have a compulsory retirement age for all employees, regardless of their competence, their passion, and the quality of their work.
- As people approach and then pass retirement age, they often have increasing difficulty finding employment.

It is important to understand the influence these restrictions have on all of us. As Martinez says, "your biology is strongly influenced by the cultural attributions (causes) you give to your actions. If you believe that you're 'too old' for something, your biology will comply."[2]

Having conversations can help you become conscious of cultural and societal influences that may affect your decisions about your Next Chapter.

EXCAVATING CULTURAL NORMS

Just imagine for a moment that you are at a social event. You have been considering retirement, and someone asks you, "What do you do? Are you retired?"

What would you say? Would you embrace the cultural concept of retirement, or would you rebel against it? We both did this exercise, and this is how each of us responded.

Gail reacted to the word *retirement*. She said, "I work part time. I don't consider myself retired. Retirement brings up the idea of losing the ability to contribute and add value. I still love what I do, and I hope to be able to continue to work for quite a while."

Marilyn answered, "No, I'm not retired. I've been trying to retire, but I haven't been very successful at it, and I've finally realized that retirement is not for me. I love what I do and have clients and colleagues I enjoy working with, so I've officially given myself permission not to retire."

Neither of us liked being pigeonholed as being retired. We wondered why we both had such a visceral reaction to the word *retirement*, just like our friend Valerie in the Introduction had. We then decided to explore the origins of retirement and the roots of the feelings and stories many of us have about retirement.

We started our exploration by looking at retirement around the world. We found in many instances that attitudes about retirement are tied to aging and the attitudes different cultures have about aging. For instance, in the West we place a high value on youth and on looking and acting young, rather than on the wisdom and experience that come with age.

Happily, we found that not all cultural norms around retirement and aging are negative, especially when we looked to the East. Asian cultures honor elders far more than is typical here in the West. Most people in Korea and China practice the Confucian principle of filial piety, or the importance of respect for your parents.[3] In Japan, one's 60th birthday, called *kanreki*, is celebrated as the start of a second childhood, a time of symbolic rebirth.[4]

In Mediterranean and Latin cultures, family is a priority, and elders are honored and respected, too. In Greece, old age is celebrated. In India, joint families are common: Several generations of families live together, and the elders are revered.

Take a moment now to consider your family background; the way you see your colleagues, friends, and neighbors retiring; and the messages you are getting from your environment regarding what a "good retirement" looks like. Do you agree with the examples you see? How do you feel about the cultural norms around you? Do you feel pressured to retire a certain way, or do you feel free to do it your own way, however that may look for you?

Let's take a look at how the modern concept of retirement came about so that we may begin unpacking the cultural norms that surround us today.

ROOTS OF RETIREMENT IN THE UNITED STATES

The notion of retirement took root in the United States when the agrarian economy gave way to the Industrial Age and factories began to replace farms.[5] During most of the 1800s, farming dominated the U.S. economy. Most men worked until their health gave out, and then they passed the heavy workload on to sons or hired hands.

With the transition from farm to factory, the workforce included a large number of older workers. Used to the norms of farming, many of these older workers refused to retire.[6] They could still work, so why would they stop?

This lack of turnover in the workforce caused significant unemployment among younger workers. The onset of the Great Depression made the situation worse by causing severe poverty among older workers as well. These older workers were the first to be laid off and the last to be called back as the economy improved.

The modern, industrialized society brought with it additional economic insecurity to many American families. This insecurity, augmented by the Great Depression, was the primary reason for the introduction of the Social Security Act of 1935.[7] By the time Franklin Delano Roosevelt introduced the idea of a social insurance program to the United States in the 1930s, more than 20 nations around the world had some type of program in effect.

> When the Social Security Act was passed, the official retirement age was 65, and the life expectancy for American men was 58.

EVOLUTION OF PENSION PLANS

During the 20th century, the idea of pensions was also growing in popularity.[8] Military pensions had long been given to soldiers. In fact, they originated in 13 B.C., when the Roman government began paying pensions to Roman soldiers who had served 20 years. In the 1500s, Britain and several other European countries offered pensions in stages, first to officers and then to enlisted men.[9]

Pensions were first offered in the American colonies in 1636, when the Plymouth Colony offered them to soldiers who were disabled defending the colony from Native Americans. During the Revolutionary War the colonies passed the first pension laws, and in 1789 the federal government assumed full responsibility for pension payments to disabled veterans.[10]

By the mid-1800s many large American cities had started giving public pensions to firefighters, policemen, and teachers. In 1875, American Express Company started the first private pension fund, and by the 1920s, many American industries were giving their workers some sort of pension.[11] Most of the programs were based on life expectancy and economics.

Many Americans now had the money to retire, but they found they still wanted something to do, so they discovered leisure. The rich discovered it first, but by the 1920s, retirement communities had started to develop. Between 1921 and 1930, the number of golf courses in the United States tripled.[12]

By the time the baby boomers were born in the 1940s and 1950s, three stages of life had emerged as the norm: education, work, and retirement. Retirement marked the end of an individual's working career and the beginning of the final phase of life.[13]

Pensions continued to become more the norm in private industry, and people enjoyed the added benefits of Social Security. In her article "The Economic History of Retirement in the United States," Joanna Short cited the disappearance of older men (over 65) from the labor force as one of the most striking changes in the American labor market that occurred in the 20th century.[14] The percentage of men 65 and older in the labor market dropped from 78 percent in 1880 to 20 percent in 1990. That trend reflected that older men expected to spend a much larger portion of their life in retirement relative to men living in the 19th century.

> In 1880, 78 percent of men 65 and older were in the labor market. By 1990, only 20 percent of men 65 and older were in the labor market.

RETIREMENT IN THE LATTER PART OF THE 20TH CENTURY

During the 1970s, cruise lines and retirement communities became increasingly popular, as more and more people looked forward to leaving the workforce for a leisurely life.[15] Today's classic concept of retirement had fully arrived: The husband leaves the workforce at 65, and the stay-at-home wife continues alongside him. They spend their days happily tending to their homes, traveling, or playing golf and card games.

According to Short, retirement is a relatively new phenomenon among women.[16] As a result, women who are contemplating retirement now might not have their mothers as role models for how to do this. Research shows that by 1940, most young women were still leaving the workforce when they married, "and only a small majority ever returned to work. Retirement was a nonissue."[17]

The number of married women in the workforce started to increase after World War II, and in 1998 research showed that the average retirement age for men and women was virtually the same. Thus, the norms of retirement continued to shift as more women entered the workforce, and the concept of the two-income family emerged.

Along with these societal changes, economic changes had started to happen. The percentage of workers covered by traditional pension plans that paid a lifetime annuity, often based on years of service and final salary, steadily declined. From 1980 through 2008, the number of private-sector workers participating in defined pension plans fell from 38 percent to 20 percent. In contrast, the percentage of workers covered by 401(k) plans grew from 8 percent to 31 percent. 401(k) plans gave the participants more control over their finances than did traditional pension plans.[18]

The traditional picture of retirement continued to change, as did the models for—and perceptions about—retirement. The norm of the working father and stay-at-home mother had shifted. The norm of retirees who played golf or traveled most of the time evolved into a new picture of retirement. People were choosing to work longer, either for financial reasons or to stay fulfilled.

THE TIMES THEY ARE A-CHANGIN'

When Bob Dylan recorded and first performed this song at a Carnegie Hall concert in 1963, it quickly became an anthem for baby boomers who wanted change of all sorts: political, social, economic, and more. Twenty years later, Steve Jobs recited the second verse of the song when opening the 1984 Apple annual shareholders' meeting and unveiling the first Macintosh computer. Now, over 55 years after the song was first performed, baby boomers are once again making changes—in how they live the last few decades of their lives. Although some still play golf and bridge like their parents did, others stay in the workforce, start new businesses, take leadership roles on boards, or go back to school.

SOCIETY'S CURRENT VIEW OF RETIREMENT

As baby boomers, our generation has opportunities our parents and grandparents never had. Retirement used to signal the beginning of the end. Now it signals the start of what can be the most satisfying and fulfilling time in our lives. Or, as Bob Buford described it in his book *Halftime*, the season of "Now what?"[19] We agree with Richard Leider and David Shapiro, who proclaimed, "We believe that the second half of life offers us unique opportunities for growing whole, not growing old."[20]

Just as baby boomers have rewritten societal rules and norms at every stage of their lives, they are now recreating retirement. In 2019 and beyond, both men and women have an opportunity to add multiple stages to their lives beyond the traditional retirement and to explore other lifestyles and choices.

People are living longer today than ever. According to the Social Security Administration, the average man who just celebrated his 65th birthday can expect to live until 84.3, and the average woman can expect to live to 86.7.[21] Also, the Social Security Administration's research predicts that one out of every four 65-year-olds will live past 90, and one out of every ten will live past 95. This means that 25 percent of baby boomers will have at least 25 more years to live after they turn 65. With all that potential time on our hands, we have the freedom to consciously create our Next Chapter rather than default to societal expectations.

> **Sixty-five-year-old men today can expect to live to 84.3.**
> **Sixty-five-year-old women can expect to live to 86.7.**

As a society, we are managing our vitality assets better today than in the past. We are more health conscious, and we are taking better care of our physical and mental well-being. Deaths from major diseases are decreasing, and people are increasingly realizing the benefits of exercise and weight control.[22] We are acknowledging aging but not letting it limit us.

We can continue to work, start a new career, pursue a passion, or take advantage of a myriad of other opportunities. Travel is a popular activity in retirement. Some retirees now have the time and the finances to see the world and travel to places they only dreamed of in the past.

Also, many retirees are hitting the open roads in RVs to see the United States and to be a part of their grandchildren's lives during important events without ever having to unpack. Sharing those key events with their family is very important to many retirees. In fact, according to the latest census, we are currently in the middle of a "grandparents boom," as a record 70 million Americans have grandchildren![23]

In *The Essential Grandparent*, Lillian Carson wrote that being in touch with the younger generation literally beefs up the immune system.[24] Barbara Graham, creator of Grandparent.com, said, "My mother loved my son, but there was nothing like the level of obsession my friends and I have for our grandchildren."[25] With four young grandchildren, Gail echoes that statement.

Many retirees volunteer for charities, community organizations, or churches. Along with continuing to work, Gail serves on the board of directors of the United Way of Metropolitan Dallas and the Children's Medical Center Foundation, while Marilyn serves on the board of the Dallas Fort Worth Humane Society.

Other people in their Next Chapter choose to go back to school, maybe to finish college or get advanced degrees but often simply for the love of learning. In many states, colleges offer reduced tuition to residents over 55 if they enroll in a class that is not already filled with students who are paying full price for the course.

Ellie Aronoff is a vibrant 92-year-old retired school teacher from New England and a former caterer to the likes of American composer Leonard Bernstein. The last time we checked in with Ellie, she was taking three college courses. Even into her 90s she still gets around by car, attends the theater, and takes herself to breakfast when she gets lonely. When guests drop in at Ellie's house, they often find her with a mischievous smile on her face and jazz or chamber music playing at high volume. Ellie embodies vitality in retirement to all who know her. Ellie's advice to others in the Next Chapter? "You are in charge of your life. You learn until you die! You just have to be curious."

Does Ellie match your expectations of what retirement looks like? Regardless of your answer, as you approach your Next Chapter, it's a great time to examine your cultural beliefs about retirement, so that you can make conscious decisions about how you want to live during this stage of life.

There are many different ways to categorize retirement options. On the basis of our conversations and research so far, we offer the following six categories for the Next Chapter.

 Traditionalist—The Traditionalist stops working and engages in a variety of nonpaid, mostly leisure activities.

 Altruist—The Altruist stops working and instead volunteers, as a board member or in other roles.

 Lifelong Learner—The Lifelong Learner stops working and pursues a nonpaid activity that requires significant practice or continued learning.

 Stair Stepper—The Stair Stepper continues to work in the same career, while gradually cutting back.

 Boomeranger—The Boomeranger takes a break and then returns to work.

Reinventor—The Reinventor continues to work in a new career or another role.

It is interesting that three out of the six choices involve working. Some people continue working because they love what they do, and others choose not to retire because they need the income. Still others return to work after retiring out of boredom; because they don't feel valued; or for social interaction, social status, or mental stimulation. According to a survey by the Transamerica Center for Retirement Studies, 66 percent of baby boomers plan to work or are already working past age 65.[26] (We provide more information on these six life-style categories in Conversation 3—Options.)

> **Sixty-six percent of baby boomers plan to work or are already working past age 65.**

A Bankrate Money Pulse Survey conducted in August 2016 by Princeton Survey Research Associates International found that only 52 percent of Americans plan to retire in their 60s and 17 percent said they want to work until death.[27] The survey also found that early retirement is not the goal it once was, as only 13 percent of the respondents said they wanted to retire in their 50s, compared with 27 percent in a 2007 survey.

Retirees have energy and ideas, and they want to make a difference. Merrill Lynch's 2016 Leisure in Retirement: Beyond the Bucket List study, conducted by Age Wave, found that retirees value fun and quality time with friends and family above all and that in 2015 they spent more on travel and leisure than any other age group.[28] The study also found that

- 88 percent of respondents viewed retirement as a new beginning instead of an ending

- 66 percent preferred to try new things rather than sticking to old hobbies or pastimes
- 95 percent preferred to purchase experiences rather than things.

As Ken Dychtwald, the founder of Age Wave and considered the "nation's foremost thought leader on aging populations," has emphasized, "we're seeing a new model of aging."[29]

Another factor enters into why some people are working longer: for the money and fringe benefits. Some find they have to continue working to be financially secure, often because they do not have sufficient savings, access to a pension, or a spouse to help share the burden of today's cost of living. Working part time or being semi-retired can also be a choice for this group. Semi-retirement gives people a chance to change their lifestyles gradually while still maintaining an income.

Concerns about the future solvency of Social Security place additional pressure on individuals deciding whether they will be able to leave the workforce when desired and collect benefits in the future. Baby boomers are retiring at a rate of 10,000 per day. Private and government pension programs might not be sufficient to support this influx, and Social Security benefits may be reduced due to a shortfall of funds.

THE INFLUENCE OF FAMILY AND FRIENDS

Along with society's view of retirement, we are influenced by our families and friends and how they approach retirement.

For example, Gail's mother was a nurse who left her career to stay home and raise a family. Her father was a successful businessman and retired in his early 60s. After her father retired, he and Gail's mom traveled, played lots of golf and bridge, had a rich social life, and spent as much time as possible with their grandchildren. They had a traditional retirement by the standards of their generation.

Reflecting on their examples, Gail realized that their decisions have affected her internal stories about retirement and what she believes she "should" and "shouldn't" do. She carries an internal story that she should retire and spend the majority of her time traveling, having fun, and enjoying her family.

Marilyn grew up in northwest Louisiana. Her mother retired at the age of 62. She had worked very hard, working four full days and two half days a week as a nurse, so after retirement, she took some time off to rest and relax. After that she settled into a retirement routine. She had lunch with friends each week, volunteered for Meals on Wheels, and visited her children and grandchildren whenever she could. Marilyn's father was a building contractor and worked until he was in his early 80s. He was also very active in the church and in a local businessmen's group.

Although the broader culture around her reflected relatively traditional southern U.S. values, Marilyn doesn't carry an internal story about whether she should or should not retire at a certain age. She realized that the examples of the different ways her parents handled retirement introduced her to the idea that she had choices regarding how and when she wanted to retire.

We also have the examples of each of our husbands to draw on. Gail's husband *Jeff Murphy* retired around the age of 63 and thoroughly loves being retired in the traditional sense. In fact, the family jokes that when he retired, Jeff started walking about two hours a day, and, as a result, his walking companion—their standard poodle—lost ten pounds.

Marilyn's husband *Brian Bushey* retired at the age of 66 and really enjoys being traditionally retired. He has a thirst for knowledge and spends most of his days researching on the computer, enjoying their condo on the lake, and serving on one of the committees of their condo association.

Watching others retire does not always put pressure on us to do it in the same way; sometimes it gives us insight into how we'd like to do things differently. As Marilyn's husband Brian explained, "I wasn't sure what I wanted to do when I retired. Watching my parents, I knew some things I didn't want to do. I observed them work very hard on our family dairy farm until they sold it, only to retire and fill their time with taking care of a home, a camp, and numerous pieces of equipment—a small tractor, a snow blower, multiple cars, and more—and I realized that was not how I wanted to spend my retirement. I wanted a simpler life."

Along with these familial examples, we have the examples of our friends, colleagues, and peers. Many of our friends are coaches and consultants who love what they do and plan to continue working past the traditional retirement age. Some have already retired and enjoy traveling. Others are approaching retirement age and are still putting children through college, so retirement is not even on their horizon. How are your friends and family retiring? How does that affect your own beliefs about retirement?

All of these cultural and familial influences shape your thoughts and ideas about retirement, whether you realize it or not. It is important to understand the effect they have on you and your choices about retirement as you begin your own journey.

CONVERSATION STARTER

A conversation is the vehicle that will steer you to an understanding of these complex influences on your thoughts about retirement. As we mentioned in the Introduction, you might have those conversations with yourself, with others, or with the universe.

Here are some thoughts to stimulate possible internal or external conversations concerning the influence that cultural, familial, and societal messages have on your vision of retirement:

- How would you describe existing cultural expectations of old age?
- What lifestyle choices did your parents and other key people in your life make when they reached their 60s and beyond?
- How have those cultural expectations and choices influenced your beliefs about retirement?

At the end of each chapter, we've included a special section called Rest Stop. When you are driving a car, you pause at a rest stop for a few minutes to put some nutrition into your body, release what you don't need, reenergize, and gain more equanimity for the next leg of your trip.

In the same way, we hope that the Rest Stop sections in this book provide an opportunity for you to reflect, revitalize, gain perspective, and possibly think "outside the box" before embarking on the next leg of your journey. We hope you enjoy these rest stops and that when you're ready, to paraphrase the words of Willie Nelson, you're anxious to be "on the road again."

This is the first rest stop in the book, and it is a quote from Carl Jung. Enjoy!

We cannot live the afternoon of life according to the programme of life's morning.

—Carl Jung, psychologist

Hurdles: Watch Out for Speed Bumps

Climb every mountain
Search high and low
Follow every byway
Every path you know

Climb every mountain
Ford every stream
Follow every rainbow
'Till you find your dream
A dream that will need
All the love you can give
Every day of your life
For as long as you live

—RICHARD RODGERS (MUSIC) AND
OSCAR HAMMERSTEIN II (LYRICS),
"CLIMB EV'RY MOUNTAIN"

HURDLES

Noticing Your Personal Beliefs and Stories That Help or Hinder You

Not long ago, we found ourselves in the midst of the following conversation.

"I was in a meeting the other day," said Gail, "and I found myself thinking, 'I'm the oldest person in the room. Do I look it? Do they know it? Do they even care?'"

Marilyn replied, "I know those stories. The other day, I was thinking some similar thoughts when, all of a sudden, someone said, 'Marilyn, what do you think about this?' Then I realized that I was caught up in my own conversation about aging while the actual conversation in the room was still going on."

"Oh yes," said Gail. "Sometimes, my internal conversations can get a bit ridiculous, and I start thinking, 'I'm not sure I remembered to put on mascara today. Oh no, I really look tired when I don't wear mascara. And when I look tired, I look older.'"

"Yes, I've been there," replied Marilyn. "The other day I was with a long-term client and I found myself thinking, 'I wonder if he notices that I'm getting older. Maybe I should retire before he realizes it.'"

Then we started laughing at ourselves, and the conversation went on.

Are we outliers when it comes to the stories we tell ourselves about what it means to get older within the workplace?

Are these internal conversations more common among women than men? Or is there something shared about these stories that reflects our collective embarrassment—or sometimes even shame—about growing older?

These stories about getting older are often really funny, and we can laugh at ourselves . . . yet they often come from a deeper set of beliefs that we have accepted as part of "what is." Many of these beliefs do not serve us or the people around us.

AGING, RETIREMENT, AND CHOICES IN THE NEXT CHAPTER

The cultural norms that we discussed in Conversation 1—Culture set the stage for the personal, internal beliefs that affect your choices during retirement. We personally find it hard to think about retirement without thinking about aging. We know there are people who can separate those concepts; however, for us, they are interconnected.

For so many people, these norms are also deeply engrained into the beliefs and actions of their family, friends, and colleagues. For example, we have noticed that many of our contemporaries also seem to carry stories about aging.

One 50-year old colleague, who leads a huge organization with many complexities, made the following comment when she forgot someone's name: "I'm forgetting things more and more as I get older." Another colleague—male—commented in a group meeting, "I'm the oldest person in the room, so I might not be up on the latest ideas." When women get together, we often talk about the physical signs of aging—and rarely with a tone of celebration.

When we look at these situations as observers, we can see the irony and the misperceptions. Our colleague who complains she's forgetting things is one of the most talented leaders we know, and she effectively juggles multiple moving parts in her professional life every day. The man who thought he was the oldest in the room provided a number of insightful and creative comments—plus, ironically, he wasn't the oldest.

As for women when we get together, perhaps we could do a better job of noticing the downward effect that these conversations have on our moods and perspectives. Perhaps we could discuss the positive aspects of aging instead—like wisdom, freedom, and courage?

Sometimes, our adult children reflect our cultural norms. Gail's daughters, Lindsey and Jaime, recently asked, "Mom, why are you still working?"

The comments made by Jaime, Lindsey, and our colleagues are examples of how cultural norms surround us. Conversation 2 is concerned with the internal stories we start to tell ourselves when we accept cultural norms that don't serve us. These internal stories then turn into hurdles that stop us from designing the Next Chapter we truly desire.

People don't necessarily adopt all of the cultural and familial views that they are exposed to, yet most of us do seem to allow some of them to seep their way into our own ways of thinking and the choices that we make. When these cultural beliefs take hold within us, they can help us, or they can hinder us. They can represent catapults for us, propelling us toward our ideal Next Chapter, or they can be hurdles for us.

DO AGING AND RETIREMENT GO HAND IN HAND?

Are our beliefs and views about aging necessarily connected to our views about retirement or what we "should do" in our Next Chapter? Some people can easily distinguish their beliefs about retirement and aging from each other because they see them as separate issues. For many of us, however, our beliefs about retirement are tightly intertwined with our beliefs about aging. Although we know intellectually that they are not one and the same, we might react emotionally to the idea of retirement primarily because we have not yet made peace with the idea of aging. In this book, we aren't trying to resolve this often complex psychological dynamic; it is, however, an area for possible introspection as you read and process this book. What are your beliefs about aging, and how do they help or hinder your ability to plan a Next Chapter that is right for you?

THE BELIEFS AND INTERNAL STORIES THAT HELP OR HINDER US

When our beliefs and stories help us, they spur our confidence, our willingness to explore options, and our courage to take less common yet more personally fulfilling paths. When these beliefs and stories hinder us, they can become big hurdles for us.

Our internal stories and beliefs can affect our choices even when we have no idea of their influence. Although we are often consciously aware of the stories we tell ourselves, sometimes we are not. Even when we don't consciously recognize the impact of our stories, they can manifest as an internal struggle, uncertainty, or subtle physical tension.

Whether or not we can articulate our stories and beliefs, they may shape our decisions about retirement, our perceptions of aging, our self-image, and our ideas about what we should do and be at this stage of life. If we don't recognize them, we can put unnecessary limitations on ourselves. Often, this means we play it safe rather than nudging ourselves out of our comfort zone.

Marilyn's comment—half joking and half serious—that maybe she should retire before her client starts to notice she's getting older is a good example of how what we tell ourselves can hold us back. Fortunately, Marilyn recognized this comment as an internal story and saw that it could be a potential hurdle if she chose to believe it.

As Eckhart Tolle stated, "The primary cause of unhappiness is never the situation, but your thoughts about it."[1] Once Marilyn recognized her thoughts—her internal story—about aging and retirement, she could rewrite it.

> **"The primary cause of unhappiness is never the situation, but your thoughts about it." —Eckhart Tolle**

In essence, internal stories are conversations we have with ourselves. Here are some other examples of stories we can tell ourselves. Do you recognize yourself in any of them?

- I'm too old to do this work anymore.
- I don't want my work colleagues to see me getting older.
- I don't remember his name. Am I losing my memory?
- I need to keep—or start—dyeing my hair because I don't want to look any older than I am.
- I'm being pigeonholed because of my age. I don't like it, but there is nothing I can do.
- I'll never learn this new technology.
- They think I'm irrelevant. Am I?
- I'm not as creative or as mentally agile as I used to be.
- I used to be excited about making changes in my life. Not anymore!
- My doctor doesn't listen to me when I say something is wrong. Is that because I'm older or because I need to change doctors?

Or maybe you've caught yourself making any variation of the following generalizations:

- Seniors should be/look like/do _____.
- I am too old to _____.
- Why would anyone want to _____?
- I'm afraid to try _____.

> Our beliefs and stories can spur our confidence, our willingness to explore options, and our courage to take less common yet more personally fulfilling paths—or they can become big hurdles for us.

CASCADING STORIES

Sometimes, one story can lead to another, and then another, and then yet another.

An often frustrating aspect of cascading stories is that they can manifest in different ways, and they can "mushroom" into more complex layers.

For example, we all have our own personal perceptions and stories. In conversation with others, we often are exposed to clues about their perceptions through their verbal comments and nonverbal reactions. Then we may form—correctly or incorrectly—our assessment of their perceptions. Going full circle, this assessment of others' perceptions may then affect the choices we make and the actions we take.

Figure 2.1 demonstrates how we can allow our personal perceptions, beliefs, and stories to mushroom into a more complex situation. When this happens, we end up allowing our stories to take up valuable real estate in our minds, and we often act in accordance with these frequently inaccurate perceptions. In essence, our stories become our reality.

A hypothetical example of this phenomenon, displayed conversation by conversation, is included in Figure 2.1. John is 65 and the CEO of a third-generation family business. All the previous family members

FIGURE 2.1: EXAMPLE CONVERSATION OF LAYERED PERCEPTIONS

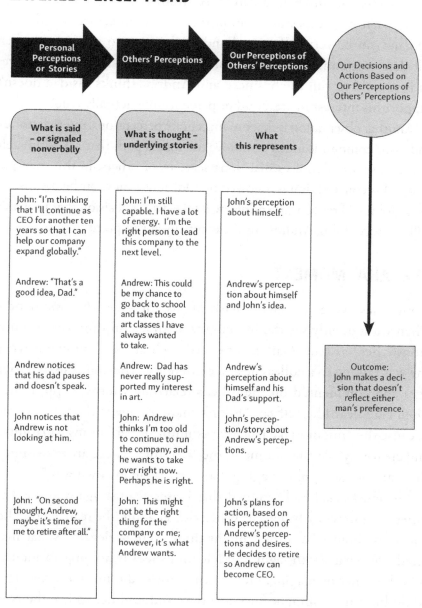

retired before they were 65 and turned the business over to the next generation. John recently engaged in the conversation shown in Figure 2.1, with his son and heir-apparent, Andrew.

So, what does this story demonstrate? One observation is that we humans can be very self-critical and easily jump to inaccurate, often self-defeating conclusions. For example, John thinks Andrew believes he is too old to run the business, and Andrew thinks his dad doesn't support his interest in art. Neither perception is actually true!

Another observation is that our inaccurate perceptions, internal stories, and poor communications can move us along a path that can ultimately lead to a series of choices that don't serve us or others. In this example, unless this conversation is followed by additional, more authentic discussions, John will retire and Andrew will take over, a decision that probably will not serve John, Andrew, or the company at this point in time.

THE "AHA" MOMENT

Sometimes, we experience a flash of insight—an "aha" moment—when we suddenly see the inaccuracy of an assumption that we previously held as true. Gail experienced such an "aha" moment when she was talking to a colleague at a conference. They both shared their ages and commented on the other's relatively youthful appearance. Then Gail heard herself say, "I don't share my age with many people, because they might make negative assumptions about my capabilities and creativity." At that moment, the "aha" hit: "Those are *my* assumptions and *my* story about aging. I am getting in my own way."

Previously Gail had assumed that biases against age were held by others, not necessarily herself. When the "aha" hit, she realized that her concerns about what others might think were irrelevant. What mattered was what *she* thought and felt, and she was holding an internal bias about her own aging. Her internal stories did not serve her. They could limit her willingness to take risks and lead her to live the Next Chapter "safer and smaller" than she truly wanted.

The reverse is also true—from time to time, almost everyone makes assumptions about others on the basis of their age. For example, on a trip we once took to the beach together, we were at the guardhouse, trying to enter. The security guard, who had gray hair and a crusty personality, looked like he was in his late 70s or early 80s, and he kept insisting that we were at the wrong gate. We argued the other way, feeling certain we had arrived at the correct spot. Eventually, we sorted out the details and realized that we were, in fact, at the wrong gate.

As we walked away, we commented to each other, "That's an example of an older person being inflexible." Then, in a flash of self-insight, we realized that we were making a judgment about this person on the basis of his age and that we were really the ones being inflexible!

To use a phrase from Judith Glaser, author of *Conversational Intelligence*, we were exhibiting an "addiction to being right."[2] We assumed that the older security guard was inflexible when we were actually demonstrating inflexibility ourselves. We wondered, if we were able to break our own assumptions about age, how might we live our lives differently?

THE ROLE OF EGO: FROM WHO'S WHO TO WHO'S THAT

A few years ago, a recently retired CEO commented to Gail, "When I retired, I went from 'Who's who' to 'Who's he?'" He seemed to take that change in stride and with a sense of humor. Still, many of us recognize that we derive a level of satisfaction from being admired, respected, and courted by others. When we retire, we are likely to receive less external admiration, and we may need to bolster our internal self-esteem.

> **When we retire, it can feel like we go from "Who's who" to "Who's that?"**

At one time, Marilyn was very active in the community she lived in, receiving many awards and acknowledgements. She cut back on her community involvement because of work demands. Six years later, she volunteered in her community again. There was a new group of volunteers by this time, and her suggestions and input didn't seem to be valued as they had in the past. She felt disrespected and wondered whether it had to do with her age; she began to tell herself stories about her value and contributions.

Fortunately, instead of allowing this internal hurdle to become a permanent roadblock that caused her to quit the organization, Marilyn decided to give the new experience time because it was for a cause she felt passionate about. In time she gained the respect of the new group. Her age hadn't been the issue at all; it was her newness to the group. If she had let her internal story stop her, she would have lost out on a meaningful opportunity to enjoy her Next Chapter.

Through the process of writing this book, we have had to face some of our own ego reactions. For example, early on, the two of us had the following conversation:

"If we write this book," Marilyn said, "you know what that means. It means we will have to go public about our ages."

"You're right," replied Gail. "The power of this book will come from our authenticity about our own feelings and thoughts about aging, retirement, and the choices we are making."

"Still, I wish there were a way around this."

"I do, too."

That sounds like a simple conversation. It was not! In fact, we had many more conversations like this—with more angst and brainstorming about how we could avoid disclosing our ages. We each realized that we were carrying a personal story that we should be able to avoid getting older—and that keeping our ages to ourselves would help us do that.

What if we did the opposite? Embraced our ages and told the world? Might that empower us?

Ultimately, we came back to the same conclusion—we needed to be open and honest about our ages. As we came to terms with our internal stories, we began to feel liberated, and we slowly began to let go of our embarrassment about aging.

In full disclosure, we are both works in progress. Although we are slowly coming to peace with our aging, we still haven't yet reached the point of fully embracing this inevitable fact of life. For example, at this writing, we are both 70. Although our stories about aging grip us at times, we also want to keep contributing in meaningful ways, and, for better or worse, we aren't ready to slow down. At the very least, our personal stories about aging are losing some of their grip on us as we become more open to speaking and sharing them.

OUR ROLE MODELS

We have been inspired by many examples of our contemporaries who have found meaning and vitality during their Next Chapter.

Spiritual teacher and life coach *Linda Brady* is a role model for the rest of us when it comes to embracing her age. She has been practicing her career for more than 40 years, and the way she celebrated her 75th birthday provides a sense of her vitality.

Standing in front of her party guests in her stylish clothes, with her gorgeous blonde hair and her twinkling blue eyes, Linda shared with the group that she would like to be the new model for what 75 can be. "Seventy-five is the new 50!" she proclaimed with confidence and gusto.

Having struggled with being overweight for much of her life, Linda is now at her lowest weight, eating healthier than ever and walking five miles a day. She is at the height of her career, embarking on writing her second book, growing her business, running regular workshops, traveling the country, and carrying a large client load.

Wayne Caskey is 81 years old and another example of vibrancy. He is a former CEO of several companies, and he has now been an executive coach to other CEOs and corporate officers for 18 years. Wayne lives in an independent living facility.

When he is in town, Wayne sings in a choir, exercises, or rides on a Maryland–Pennsylvania bike trail. At other times, he travels nationally to meet with his clients. He describes why he continues to work as follows: "I have real purpose in my life. I help people help themselves. I get to contribute across a broad array of businesses. Why would I retire? I will do this as long as I am physically able."

While traveling, Gail and Jeff recently met *Margie Herring* and her daughter, *Carolyn Carson*. Margie and Carolyn are 94 and 72 years old, respectively, and they both look—and act—as if they were 20 years younger. Margie and her husband owned a ranch and a farm machinery dealership. They never even talked about retiring. At 85, Margie's husband fractured his hip, yet he still drove a tractor. In fact, Carolyn tells a story about finding him driving the tractor one day—with Margie pruning trees while perched high up in the tractor's bucket. As Margie said, "Now that I'm 94, I don't do that anymore, but I did at age 80."

It wasn't until two years ago, to the dismay of her grandchildren and great-grandchildren, that Margie finally announced to her very large family (50 people and growing) that she would no longer host the family Christmas. She had hosted all the way into her 90s, and now she felt it was getting to be an imposition for some to attend since they had so many other family events. Carolyn added, "She has an amazing life and spirit."

In addition to keeping her body active with projects, gardening, trips, and doing things for others, Margie keeps her mind active with weekly trips to the library, interest in world events, and conversations with her family. She offered the following advice: "Stay involved. Be interested in what's going on. Don't just sit down. It's easy to get sedentary. The key is connection to the people you love." Margie is definitely a model for her advice.

We don't all have to be near superhuman like Linda, Wayne, or Margie. Still, they are reminders of how good it can look and feel to embrace your age with the highest vision for what you can be. These individuals in their Next Chapter are all vibrant, fit, joyful, and engaged full-tilt in their lives—they seem to radiate from their insides out into the world.

TRANSFORMING HURDLES INTO OPPORTUNITIES

Our beliefs and the impact that they have on us represent a complex constellation, and each of us carries our own variation of this constellation. Some of these beliefs are on the surface, and we see them easily, while others are deeply engrained in our value systems. Nonetheless, once we are aware of them, our stories and beliefs about aging and retirement can be shifted from hurdles into opportunities.

Your task now is to acknowledge your stories without resisting them and to remind yourself of the benefits of your current stage of life. When needed, you can seek out counseling or coaching of some type. You can also focus on practices that help to calm you and bring a sense of gratitude. Some of these practices include regular exercise, meditation, and yoga. Throughout this book, we highlight a number of mind–body methodologies that might be helpful as you navigate specific hurdles and enhance your overall quality of life.

What follows is a tool for transforming your own internal hurdles into opportunities for your Next Chapter. Typically, most of us consider internal hurdles to be beliefs or stories that are not serving us and that we want to release. These internal stories can also be thought of as conversations with ourselves. In some cases, hurdles can be deeply ingrained, hard-to-break habits.

For the purposes of this exercise, we have primarily used the term *beliefs and stories* or just *stories*. Please feel free to replace these with other related words, like *assumptions*, *expectations*, or *perceptions*.

The following exercise incorporates the mantra that we discussed in the Introduction: *Let go of your stories. Add your dreams. Keep exploring.*

As you are aware, the first two conversations of the CHOICES

Map—Culture and Hurdles—focus largely on the choices relating to letting go of your stories. This exercise provides an opportunity to identify unwanted stories and practice letting them go.

For each step within this exercise, we have also given you an example (in italics) of how Marilyn used this exercise to address one of her stories about retirement.

Step 1: Notice and Identify Your Personal Beliefs and Stories About Retirement and Aging

- When you were growing up, what decisions did your relatives and close friends make when they reached retirement age?
- What stories are you telling yourself about your own retirement and about aging in general?
- What story do you want to focus on first?

In the coaching world, there is a common-sense adage: "Fifty percent of change is awareness." This means that if you know which personal stories represent hurdles to your ongoing contribution and sense of fulfillment, then you are halfway to success in letting them go. Some stories will come to you easily, often because those are the norms followed in your family.

Marilyn chose to focus on the story she was telling herself that her husband, who is retired, wanted her to stop working so she could spend more time with him.

Step 2: Explore How Your Selected Belief or Story Serves—and Does Not Serve—You

- What thoughts, emotions, and body sensations come up when you think about this story?
- Do you feel energized or de-energized?

- As you reflect on what you care most about, do you want to keep this story, let it go, or rewrite it?

From an intellectual basis, notice how your current story hinders you and how a new one could help you. From an emotional basis, notice, without judgment, whether the current story triggers strong emotions that do not serve you. Also, notice whether a new story might allow your heart to expand with a greater sense of peace and joy. From a physical basis, notice body sensations, such as tightening feelings in specific locations, like your gut, your chest, your neck, or your eyes.

Marilyn realized that if she retired, she would have to give up work that energizes her and brings her joy. She was not energized by the idea of retiring at this point, and she experienced a sense of heaviness when she thought about it. At the same time, she wanted to spend more time with her husband. So she decided that she wanted a new story.

Step 3: Let Go of or Rewrite the Old Belief or Story, and Articulate and Embrace a New Story

- In order to let go of or rewrite the old story, what actions do you want to take? Are there conversations you want to have? Would a ritual help you to let the story go?
- How do you want to articulate your new story? Does it reflect your dreams?
- What commitment will you make to sustain your new story?

In the shamanic world, a common ritual for letting go is to write the old story or belief on a sheet of paper. Take a moment to honor it and the value it has provided. Then release it by throwing it into a fire or burying it underground.

This may be the time to acknowledge the value that the old belief or story has served. For example, one client commented, "I thought I would retire at 65, and that helped me maintain energy and momentum during some intense times. Now that I'm that age, I realize that I don't want to retire. I do, however, want something different, and I'm okay about that."

Marilyn used this process and realized she was telling herself that she should retire to spend more time with her husband, who had retired several years earlier. She had a conversation with him and found he actually enjoyed having time alone to research on the computer and to putter around their condo. When she realized this, she gave herself permission to continue doing the work she loves. She felt as if a great weight had been lifted off her shoulders.

Marilyn's new story includes fulfilling work plus more time with her husband. She now takes off most Friday afternoons to spend with him. She embraced her new story, declared to her friends and family that she loves what she does, and gave herself permission not to retire!

As Dr. Wayne Dyer so aptly phrased it, when you "change the way you look at things, the things you look at change."[3]

Some of your stories might have become old friends. Even if they don't serve you well, you are comfortable with them, and they have served a purpose for you. Letting them go might be more painful or harder than you expected. Remember to be gentle and compassionate with yourself.

Gail, for example, can be particularly hard on herself. It helps her to ask herself, "What would I say to a client, dear friend, or family member who is experiencing this challenge?"

As you move through this journey, remind yourself that this is not a "one and done" process. Stories can have many layers. You might find that as soon as you uncover and replace a story, it comes back to punch you in the gut, even though you thought you were done with it. Or you might realize that there is another story buried beneath it. Your challenge is to remain open to letting these stories surface and to commit to working through them. When you do, your ideal Next Chapter is waiting for you!

CONVERSATION STARTER

- What are the limiting beliefs and stories that you carry about retirement?
- What, if anything, is preventing you from letting these stories go?
- What new stories could you write to open up more possibilities?

"Step out of the history that is holding you back. Step into the new story you are willing to create."

—Oprah Winfrey, media executive and philanthropist

Options:
Choose Your Route

I can see clearly now, the rain is gone,
I can see all obstacles in my way
Gone are the dark clouds that had me blind
It's gonna be a bright (bright), bright (bright)
sunshiny day.
Look all around, there's nothin' but blue skies

—JOHNNY NASH, "I CAN SEE CLEARLY NOW"

OPTIONS

Stepping Up to Your Personal Power and Making a Choice

Now we approach Conversation 3—Options, the first turning point in your journey to the Next Chapter. This is the time in the CHOICES Map when you step into your power and make a commitment to live the next phase of life in a way that fits your unique sense of personal purpose. Will you continue working? Start a new business? Reduce your workload to spend more time with family? Leave the workforce altogether? Volunteer for an organization you care about? Or go back to school?

Options can be overwhelming, but they can also be empowering. They tell you that you have an array of choices in your Next Chapter beyond the traditional forms that usually are associated with the word *retirement*. They remind you that each one of us can make a personal decision regarding how we want to live out these next years, in ways that fulfill us and keep us feeling alive and energized.

In your Next Chapter, you are free to redesign your life. The choices that you make at this stage of life have the potential to expand you and help you live with vitality, enthusiasm, and joy. Ideally, your choices will also nudge you a bit out of your comfort zone.

> **The choices that you make at this stage of life have the potential to expand you and help you live with vitality, enthusiasm, and joy.**

LETTING GO OF YOUR STORIES: CONVERSATIONS 1 AND 2

At this point, you have completed the first two conversations of the CHOICES Map, and you have begun to let go of the beliefs and stories that no longer serve you. In Conversation 1—Culture, you reflected on what retirement norms and practices you inherited from your culture and family. In Conversation 2—Hurdles, you reflected on the stories that you might have previously accepted as true for yourself, and you identified the stories that you will let go or rewrite.

ADDING YOUR DREAMS: OPTIONS = OPPORTUNITIES

Now you are reaching a turning point. It's time to choose your direction for the Next Chapter. During Conversation 3—Options, you will begin the process of adding your dreams so that you can make a decision that reflects the best of who you are and the best of who you want to be.

The Options conversation is a choice point where you sort through the opportunities before you, focus on the option or options that best meet your goals, and make a decision regarding your next steps. Notice the word *opportunities*. Just as the *O* in the CHOICES Map stands for *options*, it stands for *opportunities*, too.

You likely have many options for how you can spend your Next Chapter. When you start to think of these options as *opportunities*, you embrace that they are more than a simple menu of choices. They are launching pads for doing something great for yourself, for your loved ones, for the world, or any combination of these.

One person's great will be different from another person's great—it may be humble, or it may be grand. The key idea is that the Next Chapter is your chance to retool, refresh, get it right, do it differently —create! The Next Chapter represents your Next Opportunity.

Even if you are limited by finances or health, you can use the ideas in this conversation to generate possibilities and to be creative—to go for what you really want, by balancing reality with possibility. For example, we recently met a man we'll call *George*, who had retired from his previous career and now works as a bellhop at a resort, primarily so that he can have access to superb golf courses with significantly reduced greens fees.

At 70 years old, *Anita* was diagnosed with an autoimmune disease called myasthenia gravis just a couple of years after her husband, Joe, retired from his career as an executive at a petroleum company. Anita found herself feeling so tired that she could hardly leave the house. Anita and Joe had recently purchased their dream retirement home in Florida and wondered what would happen to their plans to enjoy life together, spend time with family, and travel the world.

While the diagnosis was scary, Anita was able to work with her physicians to get her disease under control through medical interventions and rest. Although she fatigues far more easily than in her younger years, Anita and Joe are living out their Next Chapter much in sync with their original plans. They enjoy their beautiful Florida home together, take a couple of international cruises each year, and spend time with their extended family throughout the year. Anita has found a way to balance reality with possibility.

REVISITING YOUR CHOICES

When it comes to selecting the right option for the Next Chapter, your choice may last for many years or for only a few months. As goals, physical health, and life circumstances change, so too may the options you choose to pursue. For example, the time may come when Anita starts taking cruises closer to home, for shorter spells, or not at all. George may stop working as a bellhop when changes in his physical health make it hard for him to play golf or carry luggage.

Most people will end up revisiting this choice point multiple times during their Next Chapter years. That's okay! As Gail's daughter, who is an early millennial, recently pointed out, it's much like how many millennials do it, looking at their career goals in increments of two to five years. They don't feel the need to stay at one organization or one job for the entirety of their careers; they are free to make moves and changes every few years.

Bev and Ray Mentzer retired from their executive engineering roles at a large oil company a few years ago. As they were looking at their options, they attended a program on retirement planning at the University of North Carolina in Asheville. There they learned that retirement will likely consist of multiple phases, such as Plan A, Plan B, maybe Plan C, and beyond.

For the Mentzers, Plan A involved Ray's teaching at Texas A&M University, while Bev focused on volunteering and supporting her aging parents. After living Plan A for a while, they moved to Plan B, which they are currently still enjoying. Ray is a visiting professor of chemical engineering at Purdue University for one semester a year.

Plan B's move to Indiana was a big change for Bev because she had never relocated without going right to work. She volunteered on campus and connected with the community to avoid loneliness and boredom. A job "found her," and she now mentors students as an industrial career counselor at Purdue as well. During the rest of the year, Bev and Ray travel and enjoy a more relaxed life in Houston.

Whether you are on Plan A, Plan B, Plan C, or beyond, the CHOICES Map can be helpful when you are ready to consider a new phase of your Next Chapter. Each time you review the map, the Options conversation is a reminder that you are making an important decision, based on your personal sense of power, capacity, and purpose at that point in time.

DEFINING THE GOOD LIFE

Before you select from your options for the Next Chapter, it helps to have an idea of what you want for yourself in this stage to come. As we have talked to our contemporaries, we have learned that our peers are having a variety of thoughts about how they want to spend the Next Chapter.

The key is to notice these thoughts, acknowledge their value, and allow them to exist while you are formulating your decision. Below is a list of possible thoughts that might come up.

- "I love what I do now. And I want to find a different way to do it."
- "I'm maxed out on my current job or profession. I want to do something different."
- "I don't plan to retire for as long as physically possible."
- "I thought I wanted to retire when I turned 65. Now that I'm there, I am reconsidering."
- "I've been offered an incredible opportunity. Do I want to keep working?"
- "I want to start a business—perhaps to help my children get on their feet. Then I can pass the business down to them."
- "I want to be on one or more paid boards."
- "I love my hobby, and I want to spend much more time on it."
- "I want a full, classic retirement. I want to enjoy this time of my life, and I don't ever want to use an alarm clock again."
- "I want to rest and rejuvenate for a while, and then maybe I will go back to work."
- "I was nudged—or forced—into retirement. What could I possibly do now?"

Many of these thoughts can be translated into a few simple statements or questions:

- "I want to spend more time with . . ."
- "I want to learn how to . . ."
- "As a child, I dreamed that someday I would . . ."
- "I find it fulfilling to . . ."

These statements are not fully formed visions of the Next Chapter; however, they are a great starting point. They are people's initial thoughts or desires regarding what they would like for the Next Chapter. What would your statements look like if you added them to this list?

It's not uncommon for people to find themselves having simultaneous thoughts—or desires—that cannot be accomplished at the same time. These simultaneous, often contradictory desires can relate to many topics. A simple example is, "I want to eat that piece of cake, and I want to lose weight." Possible Next Chapter examples are, "I want to downsize, and I want to have enough room when my family comes to visit," or, "I want to make some additional money, and I would love to be free each day to do what I want."

How should you deal with these potentially contradictory desires? Although there is no magic right answer, it often helps to notice the thoughts and ask, "Is one desire more important or urgent than the other? Could I allow myself to hold a space for both these thoughts? Is there a way I could achieve both?" As you wrestle with the answers to these questions, you are working your way toward defining what the good life means to you.

Bob Dunham, the founder of the Institute for Generative Leadership and one of Gail's teachers and mentors, emphasizes the importance of defining, designing, and living the good life. When you contemplate your options for the Next Chapter, we encourage you to imagine your own good life. Dream a bit about what's important to you, the lifestyle you want to live, the people you want to be with, and the feelings you want to have. For example, you might want to think of your good life as living the life you want, in a mood of gratitude, with people you love and appreciate.

Bob Dunham suggests that when you are defining your good life, it is often helpful to begin with a critical question: What do you care about—what really matters to you? While you are exploring this question, we encourage you to think broadly about all aspects of your life, including relationships, service to others, work, other forms of mental challenge, spiritual beliefs, financial stability, and physical well-being. Ask yourself, "How do I take care of what I care about? What brings meaning and aliveness to me?" The good life will be very personal to you.

> **When you are defining your good life, it is often helpful to begin with a critical question: What do you care about—what really matters to you?**

TIMING

As you define what the good life means to you, consider timing. The timing of your choices for retirement—or your Next Chapter—may span a number of years. Although these timeframes apply primarily to individuals who are retiring from paid work, they can also apply to anyone who is contemplating a Next Chapter.

In our conversations and reading, we have found that there are three major timeframes to consider:

- Mid-career actions that set the stage for later retirement choices
- Decisions made within two to three years of retirement
- Periodic review and refinement during retirement.

Although these three timeframes might help you think about this subject, in reality, every individual has a unique process.

Mid-Career Actions That Set the Stage for Later Retirement Choices

Most of us believe that it is a smart practice to begin financial planning far in advance of retirement. Additionally, we are learning that many people make mid-career decisions that set the stage for a smooth professional transition into their Next Chapter.

Some people give time to their alma mater or favorite nonprofits as a way to give back and, as an added benefit, expand their networking. Some go back to school and earn higher level degrees so that they can be positioned to teach at the university level. We have a number of coaching colleagues who earned their coaching certifications while still employed, so that they could be positioned to open a coaching business sometime in the future.

While writing this book, Gail realized that she had made a key decision 20 years earlier. When she was in her mid-40s, her husband received a job offer in Dallas. They decided he should accept the job, so Gail left the corporate world in Miami and established a consulting business in Dallas. At the time, she thought about her decision primarily as a way to be with her daughters on a more flexible schedule and to allow more time to attend various personal development programs. Over time, she increasingly recognized that this decision had set the stage for her to work longer—with more flexibility in her schedule—than probably would have been possible if she had stayed in the corporate world.

Cathy Helmbrecht is a partner in a global professional services firm. Her organization sponsors several retirement planning programs for partners five or more years before expected retirement. These programs cover a variety of topics, including financial preparation, mental and emotional preparation, wellness, and lifestyle planning.

Cathy offered the following thoughts: "These programs are pushing my husband and me to discuss and update our expected retirement goals in multiple areas, including financial well-being, planned retirement activities, and health. They are also helping me think about where I want to contribute my time and resources when I retire, as well as how I can adopt daily habits to stay energized, flexible, and mindful."

When asked about her advice for others, Cathy added, "The most important learning I can share with others is to plan thoroughly—don't go cold turkey into retirement. For myself, I have been with this organization for 33 years, and it's a big part of who I am. I am aware that retirement can be an emotional experience. I'm thinking about what's important to me, where I get my energy, what I like to do, how I want to spend my days, and how I will keep connected."

Decisions Made Within Two to Three Years of Retirement

This is the timing people typically think about when they are considering their lifestyle choices for the Next Chapter. Although they might have considered their choices previously, their "serious" planning often begins when the time gets closer.

The CHOICES Map is a particularly valuable tool at this point, largely because it helps people crystallize their thinking and identify the actions needed to begin their Next Chapter in life.

Some people make choices about their timing after an unexpected or emotional event in their lives. For example, *Debbie Taylor*, a banking executive, had planned to retire in a couple of years; however, her sister passed away suddenly and unexpectedly. Debbie reconsidered her timing and retired a few months later.

As she said, "My sister's death shifted everything for me. I want to focus more on my family, my friends, and the community organizations to which I am committed." Debbie's community commitment runs deep. She is a past chair of the United Way of Metropolitan Dallas board of directors and the current chair of the board for the Dallas County Community College District Foundation.

Periodic Review and Refinement During Retirement

The beauty of the CHOICES Map is that you can use it over and over once you have entered this stage of life.

The fact is that your decisions today may work for you for only a short period of time. Your life circumstances or your mindset may shift, and you may want to make new choices based on your circumstances at a later time. You might have grandchildren, or physical issues might affect your mobility and health, or you might want to travel as much as you can while you are still physically able. When these shifts occur, you may want to adjust how you work and play.

Largely because many people will remain healthy and vital for 25 or more years after the age of 65, it's inevitable that most of us will revisit and revise our retirement plans many times during our Next Chapter. In essence, we redefine our personal definition of "the good life" over and over.

> The fact is that your decisions today may work for you for only a short period of time. Your life circumstances or your mindset may shift, and you may want to make new choices.

RETIREMENT REBELS: HAVE IT YOUR WAY

When making a lifestyle choice for your Next Chapter, now is the time to be a rebel. Rebels do not follow standard norms or rules concerning what they should or shouldn't do. Rebels decide for themselves, and they stand up for what they think is right. This is not your parents' retirement. You get to design the ideal Next Chapter for you.

The number of available lifestyle options during the traditional retirement years has grown tremendously over the past few decades. Looking forward, the options will undoubtedly continue to increase in number, and our contemporaries will find more and more ways to contribute during this stage of life.

In Conversation 1—Culture, we introduced six lifestyle categories—or distinctions—that we have identified during our conversations and research. Their purpose is to help stimulate your thinking and creativity so that you can design your Next Chapter to meet your needs, desires, and capabilities.

Although we describe these categories primarily from the point of view of people who retire from paid work outside the home, they also apply to people who shift their focus from nonpaid work inside the home to another option as their goals or the needs of their families change.

These categories are not completely distinct areas. Most retired individuals fit into two or even three categories at the same time. Likewise, although we are offering fun, easy-to-remember code names for each category, the code names are not 100 percent descriptive of each category.

 Traditionalist—The Traditionalist stops working and engages in a variety of nonpaid, mostly leisure activities

 Altruist—The Altruist stops working and instead volunteers, as a board member or in other roles

 Lifelong Learner—The Lifelong Learner stops working and pursues a nonpaid activity that requires significant practice or continued learning

 Stair Stepper—The Stair Stepper continues to work in the same career, while gradually cutting back

 Boomeranger—The Boomeranger takes a break and then returns to work

Reinventor—The Reinventor continues to work in a new career or another role.

In the pages that follow, we explore how each option for the Next Chapter might look, so you can start to try these options on for size. Discovering that an option *isn't* for you can be helpful, too, by offering a simple process of elimination that ultimately may guide you toward the best answer for you.

As you read the individual stories and experiences that follow, you might be tempted to conclude that these folks are the "lucky ones"— the people who are healthy and who do not have to worry about their financial well-being, now or in the future. To the contrary, when we talked to these individuals, we found that many of them had experienced major health issues that grabbed their full attention for a period of time. Additionally, they all emphasized that they made their lifestyle choices in the context of their financial planning and with full awareness of what they needed for their financial stability. Once they had established a financial foundation, they were then able to follow their hearts, incorporate their ongoing financial needs into their lifestyle choices, and become Retirement Rebels.

TRADITIONALIST: "ADVENTURE AWAITS!"

The Traditionalist stops working and engages in a variety of nonpaid, mostly leisure activities. This option is the closest to what people typically think of as "normal" retirement. We all know many examples of people who stop working and then fill their days with a variety of wonderful leisure activities, such as enjoying family and friends, playing or watching sports, traveling, doing crossword puzzles, connecting on social media, and playing games such as bridge or Words With Friends.

You may be thinking that a Traditionalist is not a rebel. In fact, Traditionalists may be rebelling against being told that they "should" work, "should" volunteer, or "should" go back to school. Traditionalists are following their own paths. Here are some examples of Traditionalists who know what they want.

Ann Saegert, a former real estate partner in a large law firm, is fully enjoying her retirement. She and her husband, who is also retired, start their day by having coffee or tea together. Then they go their separate ways until around 4:30 or 5:00 in the afternoon. "We thought we would downsize when we retired," Ann shared. "However, eventually, we realized that we needed more room in the house than ever, so that we could each enjoy our individual hobbies and interests."

Ann describes retirement in this way: "It's like peeling an onion. You think you are there, and then you peel another layer. I don't give anyone advice unless they ask for it. As in playground politics, I know that it's time to get out of the way and give someone else a turn. It's profoundly freeing. I listen more deeply, and my daily interactions are more satisfying. I have time to try new things that I don't do well. It's more fun than I've ever had."

Don Teeples retired at 62 after flying for 40 years. He was a pilot in the Air Force for six years, then he was a corporate pilot, and finally he became a pilot for one of the major commercial airlines. He saw many of his fellow pilots leave flying as a profession and continue flying as a hobby. During his career, he felt he had been lucky enough to find a hobby he loved and employers who would pay him for doing it; however, he wanted to retire and walk away from flying.

Don said lots of people don't consider retirement until later in life, but he started thinking and planning for it when he was about 30. He planned well and was able to retire when he met and married Deb, a woman whom he loved more than flying and wanted to spend his time with.

Don was happy to have had a career that allowed him the freedom to travel, as he says he and Deb are nomads. "We like to go, be, but not stay." Their favorite place to travel is Belize; it is their sanctuary. Their other travels have included France and Germany. As Civil War buffs, they have traveled to over 50 battlefields and along the way have made friends with two famous living civil war historians, Edwin Bearss and Thomas Cartwright.

Don says, "When we are young, we search for happiness in external things, and, as we grow older, we are more spiritually focused; memories and relationships become more important than material things."

As we mentioned in Conversation 1—Culture, Marilyn's husband Brian and Gail's husband Jeff are both happily retired from their corporate roles and spend most of their days as Traditionalists doing whatever gives them pleasure. In Brian's case, that includes spending lots of time on his computer researching every conceivable topic of interest to him—cars, politics, travel, and anything that piques his interest, whether it's something he's read about or heard on television or something he heard in a casual conversation. In Jeff's case, a pleasurable retirement means walking with Brisby, the labradoodle, two hours a day, reading multiple books a week, collecting wine, and running miscellaneous errands.

These Traditionalists were ready for a clean break from their previous work life. Their slogan might be, "Adventure awaits!"

ALTRUIST: "I LOVE TO SERVE!"

The Altruist stops working and volunteers as a board member or in other roles, mostly for nonprofit organizations. This category includes unpaid volunteer activities, usually for a cause that the individual is passionate about. As we mentioned earlier, such service is often combined with other categories. The volunteer work can encompass a variety of arenas, including nonprofit social service agencies, schools, churches, and museums.

For example, *Eric Anderson* retired from his role as an aviation executive and now volunteers as a docent several days a week at the Frontiers of Flight Museum, where he can continue his lifelong love of "all things aviation." His passion began in his childhood, when he and his dad, an aerospace engineer, would sit on their back porch and identify the types of airplanes flying over their family home.

Bill Helmbrecht, a former finance executive, grew up in Dallas and has strong Texas roots. In his retirement, he is expressing his love for history and the Dallas community through his long-term involvement as a board member and chairman of the board for the Dallas Historical Society.

Pat Bonds retired as chairman of the Dallas office of a national insurance brokerage firm. For the first few years of his retirement, he explored his love of art (painting) and remodeling homes. He bought and remodeled a house in New Mexico as a second home. He also purchased, remodeled, and flipped several other homes. Now he is demonstrating his altruistic leanings as the mayor of his community in Hideaway, Texas.

When *Charley Kienzle* retired at the age of 55, he and his wife, Carrie, executed their long-planned retirement move to Apalachicola, Florida. They began traveling extensively and pursuing other personal goals and activities, including civic involvement in this small community of 2,500. Now, a decade later, they are happy to devote a chunk of their available time to grandparenting.

Charley now primarily volunteers with a locally based organization with far-reaching impact. As president of the Apalachicola Riverkeeper, he works to further their mission of stewardship: protecting and restoring the UNESCO-designated international biosphere reserve that is the Apalachicola River ecosystem. Charley stated, "It's very fulfilling to be available to do a myriad of projects related to local community needs."

Some Altruists focus on giving back in the context of their own families, often to elderly parents, grandchildren, or other relatives and close friends. When *Mike Sharry* moved from full-time to part-time work as a wills and trusts attorney, he was able to devote more time to helping his elderly parents and aunts navigate a host of later life challenges. For example, he and his siblings have helped their parents with such activities as moving to different residences, handling finances, driving to medical appointments, and managing medications—not to mention the extraordinary value of being available to share meals and have good conversations.

These Altruists have "giving back" in their blood. Their slogan might be, "I love to serve!"

LIFELONG LEARNER: "TO LEARN IS TO LIVE!"

The Lifelong Learner stops working and pursues a nonpaid activity that requires practice or continued learning. Like the Traditionalist and the Altruist, the Lifelong Learner is involved in unpaid activities. In addition, this category often involves continued education or a level of intensity and striving that is somewhat similar to preretirement life. Examples include immersing oneself in a hobby, returning to school for another degree, practicing diligently to master a musical instrument or a new language, and entering into athletic or other types of competitions.

Shirley Anderson is pursuing her passion for gardening. She studied to be a Master Gardener, a four-month-long, intense learning process that included reading, tests, one day a week of classroom training, volunteer hours, and on-the-job practice. Now she volunteers her time as a coordinator of other Master Gardeners. Also, she recently volunteered to update the Master Gardener website, a task that essentially turned into the equivalent of a full-time job for four months.

Mary Ellen and Bill England have both retired from their long-term professions and now are enjoying a life involving travel, sewing (for Mary Ellen), and participation in various community committees. Both Lifelong Learners, they are currently taking Spanish classes at a local college. Once they have a basic understanding of the Spanish language, they plan to enroll in a month-long Spanish education and immersion program in Buenos Aires. This program will involve living with an Argentinian family and taking six classroom hours of Spanish a day.

Noel Hensley, a former partner in a large law firm, is now traveling and studying mosaic art and Islamic geometric and biomorphic art. She recalls from her trial work that different people often saw the same event in very different ways, some not registering things that indisputably were right in front of them. "I've looked at my exploration of art as a way to focus on my own visual intake and to explore new ways of seeing things," Noel said. "It feels like I'm uncovering a part of me that I'd not realized before."

Noel combines her study of Islamic art with her love of travel. Recently she went to Marrakesh with a study group to learn the geometry that underlies specific art patterns. Each day the group visited ancient sites in the city and saw the same geometric patterns that had been created hundreds of years before. "It's been an engrossing way to approach travel and appreciate the cultures in that area of the world," Noel told us.

Discussing her choice of study, Noel offered the following thoughts: "In considering retirement, I knew I wanted to use this next part of my life in an authentic manner. I'd begun by asking myself what could I do that would be different but would have similar attributes to what I'd valued in my professional life. But I found a more constructive approach for me was to think more deeply about how I could find new areas that were likely to interest and challenge me, and that I didn't yet understand. In meeting that test, every experience exposes a new part of me."

These Lifelong Learners are hungry for more. They are serial learners. Their slogan might be, "To learn is to live!"

STAIR STEPPER: "ONE STEP AT A TIME!"

 Stair Stepping is an interesting lifestyle choice that many people are now making in the Next Chapter. Stair Steppers continue to work in the same career, while gradually cutting back the amount of time they spend at work. Often, there are multiple "steps" in the process.

Both of us are examples of stair stepping. We each have our own company that provides executive coaching and consulting services. Over the last couple of years, we have pulled back a bit in order to allocate more time to our families, to our volunteer passions, and to this book.

Cheryl Cummings has stair stepped several times. She began her nursing career as a lieutenant in the Air Force, helping to evacuate the wounded out of Vietnam during the war. After her discharge, she worked as a school nurse and as a hospital staff nurse. Once she reached retirement age, she stair stepped from full time to part time. Later she stair stepped again to an "as needed" role. Even after she fully retired, she enjoyed nursing so much that she became a volunteer at the local hospital.

Phil Davis has been stair stepping via a deliberate, multi-year process as he transitions from the role of managing partner of a consulting firm that he co-founded. First he moved to a different location, where he works remotely most of the time. Over the past two to three years, he has gradually turned over many of his responsibilities to his designated successors. Additionally, each year, he has reduced the number of hours that he works.

In the meantime, Phil and his wife have traveled extensively and enjoyed their life near Austin, Texas. Of course, those of us who know Phil expect that, in the future, he will embark on additional projects, possibly as an Altruist, Lifelong Learner, or Reinventor. As he says, "I don't know yet what my Next Chapter is going to be, but I want it to be something that is intellectually engaging. I can't under any circumstance see myself just retiring."

Dr. Sheri Lewis is currently stair stepping as a naturopath. After running a thriving business for several decades, she has reduced her number of clients, reformulated her business model, and moved to a new location. Describing the benefits of her current lifestyle, she states,

"My reduced workload allows for a wonderful balance between my family and the work I love. The best of both worlds!"

These Stair Steppers like to move toward retirement in small increments. Their slogan might be, "One step at a time."

BOOMERANGER: "I KEEP BOUNCING BACK!"

The Boomeranger retires, takes a break from work, and then returns to work at a later point in time. Reflecting on the increasingly large number of people who choose this option, *the Wall Street Journal* reported, "Retirement should be called a sabbatical."[1]

The decision to return to work can come from a variety of factors, ranging from a desire to have more social interaction, to be more challenged intellectually, or to earn supplemental income. Regardless of the reasons, this phenomenon is increasingly common.

When individuals return to work, they have choices. They may elect to return to work in the same career (or careers) they had previously, or they may choose to start a new career. Similarly, they may opt to work part time or full time.

Graceanna Jones worked in the oil and gas industry for most of her career. She initially retired at age 57 and embarked on a lifestyle similar to that of a Lifelong Learner, filling her days with adventure, laughter, and learning. For seven years, she traveled the world. She learned to speak Italian, perfected her culinary skills, and volunteered for several charities in her community. She then accepted a three-month consulting assignment, which eventually grew into full-time employment where she has remained for the past five years.

As Graceanna says, "Working full time stimulates me intellectually, gives me the comradery with colleagues that I enjoy, and provides structure to my day. Mostly, though, I enjoy the experience of sharing with other people the professional knowledge I've acquired over the course of my career. I continue to learn new things almost every day.

Why would I stop working? I love the benefits I receive from giving to others and learning from them."

Chet Curtis is a two-time Boomeranger. When he was 64 years old, Chet retired for the first time, from his role as president of a Swedish software company's U.S. organization. Shortly thereafter, he received an offer to join an industry-leading software company in the education market as a senior vice president, a job that involved leading a national sales team, around-the-clock interactions with customers, and weekly travel.

When he was 69, Chet retired for the second time, at which point he embraced the lifestyle of an Altruist. He focused on a family health issue and also served as president for his local Rotary Club, college alumni association, and neighborhood homeowners' association.

After two years of retirement, Chet became a two-time Boomeranger when he received another "offer he couldn't refuse" from a consulting group that agreed to meet his conditions, including manageable travel. Chet explained his decision to leave his second retirement and "boomerang" back to work as follows: "I went back to work because I missed the interactions with team members and the partnerships and relationships with clients." After enjoying his latest job for a few more years, he has now retired for the third time at the age of 75. We all wonder: Will he be a Boomeranger again at some point in the future?

Tom Degnan retired in 2014 after spending most of his career as a chemical engineer and executive, primarily in the oil and gas industry, where, among other roles, he was responsible for partnerships with organizations focused on breakthrough technologies. He is well known in his field as an expert in zeolite catalysts, and he has written two books on the subject.

After a few months of retirement, Tom joined the faculty of the University of Notre Dame as a professor in the Department of Chemical and Biomolecular Engineering. Reflecting on his second career, Tom shared that he is energized by "interacting with the students, providing a real-world perspective to the next generation, and helping them learn how to build high-performing teams. When I left school, I never thought about teaching. When I was still in industry, a colleague and I developed and ran a semi-annual course on teams, R&D management, and leadership. Through this program, I was able to experiment with teaching, and I learned that I loved helping others be successful in organizations."

Tom offered the following advice to those who are nearing retirement: "Plan your next career thoughtfully, and experiment, if possible, within the confines of your existing career—before you pull the rip cord. Involve your partner early in your planning. Go slow initially, and take a pronounced break before you take on too many new responsibilities. Draw upon your mentors for advice and support. All people need mentors, even if you are fully retired. This is an opportunity to focus on things that bring you joy, meaning, and satisfaction."

These Boomerangers experience new job opportunities as magnets. They like to work, and they like to have some time off. Their slogan might be, "I keep bouncing back!"

REINVENTOR: "BRING IT ON!"

The Reinventor continues to work by embarking on a new career. This category involves paid work—part time or full time—in a new profession. In this category, we include becoming an entrepreneur as well as joining a corporate board of directors or any other board that pays its members rather than enlisting volunteers.

Margie Skaggs, a former corporate trainer and a Lifelong Learner, is pursuing her passion around pottery in her Next Chapter. Her interest in pottery was sparked when she began taking classes several years before she retired. Over time, she continued to build her expertise as she learned and practiced new approaches. She has now built a thriving business around her pottery that keeps her busy meeting the demands of her customers. In her Next Chapter, Margie has become an entrepreneur and a Reinventor. "I feel so fortunate to have discovered something I love doing that others also appreciate," she says.

Bob Salerno spent the majority of his career first as an executive in large retail companies and then as a consultant to the retail industry. Since he retired, he has been able to focus more time on his passion for mountain hiking, primarily in the Berkshire Hills of western Massachusetts. He became a town historian, chairs the town's finance committee, and serves on the board of three nonprofit organizations.

Additionally, Bob reinvented his lifestyle by accepting a position as a professor at the Fashion Institute of Technology in New York City, where he helps his students build expertise in the business and leadership aspects of the retail industry. Of course, many of Bob's friends are still trying to reconcile the concept of "fashion" with the image of Bob after several days of camping!

Beverly Goulet, a former airline executive, retired about a year and a half ago, and she has settled into a reinvention lifestyle that involves a mix of business focus, nonprofit contribution, and personal fun. From the business perspective, she is a member of two corporate boards of directors. One board is for a global, publicly held company in the power systems industry. This is a complex business that is currently transforming to more electrification and digitization. The second board is for a hotel real estate investment trust that owns multiple hotels across the United States. When asked what she loves about sitting on these boards, Bev answered, "The intellectual challenge of continual learning and the opportunity to interact with accomplished, interesting people with different skill sets, life stories, and points of view."

Bev is also deeply involved with the nonprofit world via organizations that represent her areas of passion: the well-being of women and girls, educational opportunities for students of limited financial resources, and research for ALS. Commenting on her choices, Bev said, "Initially, I was concerned about getting the balance right. Now I'm more comfortable with the balance. It allows me enough time to feel that I'm doing a good job with my commitments, while having time for fun, travel, and leisure."

These Reinventors love change and a challenge. Their slogan could be, "Bring it on!"

MOVING TO THE GOOD LIFE: HOW DO I CHOOSE FROM ALL MY OPTIONS?

Quite possibly, the examples listed in this chapter have triggered some reactions and stimulated some ideas about your first or next step. You might feel excited or even a bit overwhelmed by the prospect of making your choice.

At this point, we suggest that you step back, look at your life from a 50,000-foot level, and clarify your vision for your Next Chapter. In Conversation 5—Course of Action, you will revisit this vision, refine it, and prepare an action plan.

Royale Scuderi, creative strategist, consultant, and writer, states that a life vision is "the greatest asset you have." She further describes the importance of having a life vision as follows:

> "Creating a vision for your life might seem like a frivolous, fantastical waste of time, but it's not: creating a compelling vision of the life you want is actually one of the most effective strategies for achieving the life of your dreams. Perhaps the best way to look at the concept of a life vision is as a compass to help guide you to take the best actions and make the right choices that help propel you toward your best life."[2]

In many ways, your vision consists of your dreams, sprinkled with a dose of practicality.

For some, the idea of creating a vision can be exciting. For others, it may feel like a waste of time or evoke a large "groan." Yet the process is actually an effective strategy to help you connect to what you care about and to set a guidepost for your choices and actions.

We offer the following ideas to help you think through the array of options you might be considering at this point in your life.

Reflect on Your Dreams, Identify Your "Sweet Spot," and Create a Preliminary Vision

A good way to begin creating your vision is to notice your wishes and dreams—your current ones as well as those of your childhood. As you do so, think about your ideal lifestyle, or your "sweet spot." Your sweet spot can be defined as the intersection of three circles—Passion, Talents, and Ideal Environment, as portrayed in Figure 3.1. Although your sweet spot is not your vision, it will help to guide you to the right vision and lifestyle choice for you.

FIGURE 3.1: IDENTIFYING YOUR SWEET SPOT FOR THE NEXT CHAPTER

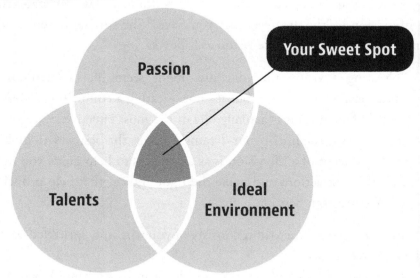

This can be a very simple step. To determine your own sweet spot, take some time to reflect on the following areas:

- **Your passion**
  - What do you care about? What brings meaning into your life?
  - What do you love to do?
  - As a child, what were your wishes and dreams? What are they now?

- **Your talents**
  - What are you good at?
  - What comes easily to you?
  - As a child, what did you do really well?

- **Your ideal environment**[3]
  - In your ideal vision, what kinds of people are in your life?
  - What does your ideal day look like?
  - Where are you geographically?
  - How are you dressed?
  - What else?

As you begin to look at the intersection of your passion, talents, and ideal environment, you will probably begin to think of several possible lifestyle choices. Some of these options could be part of your Plan A. Some may be part of your Plan B, C, or beyond. You also may have other ideas that you want to explore further, possibly in conversation with yourself or others.

When you are ready, we suggest that you write or draw a simple vision statement. Your vision statement will probably be a short, elevator-pitch-type summary that highlights your lifestyle choices and describes your "good life" in the Next Chapter.

There are no rules about what makes a good vision; everyone's vision is personal. Therefore, we encourage you to focus on finding the vision that works for you! One of the best ways to determine whether you have the "right" vision for you is to step back, take a breath, and check in with yourself internally. Does this feel right? Check with your gut, your heart, and your mind.

Since this is your vision, can you picture it? Can you see yourself living this life? Can you visualize the details? Can you hear, taste, smell, and touch this vision?

Although many people elect to write their vision in words, some prefer to display their vision graphically, perhaps as part of a vision board, a beloved photograph, or even a clip from a magazine. Again, it's your vision. When your instincts say yes, you know it's right for you.

As an example, let's look at our friend, whom we will call *Emily*. Emily retired from a demanding job with extensive travel. She identified the following components of her three circles.

- Passion: Family, especially grandchildren; having new experiences; contributing to the community
- Talents: Leadership, project management, ability to connect to people, resiliency, flexibility
- Ideal environment or lifestyle: Relaxed lifestyle, flexible day, close friends and family nearby.

When Emily looked at the connections across her three circles, she asked herself, "What lifestyle choices would support my sweet spot? What is my vision for my good life?"

Emily knew that there were probably several different lifestyle choices that were consistent with her sweet spot. As she continued to reflect, she realized that she was primarily interested in a lifestyle that was a combination of a Traditionalist and an Altruist role. From this realization, she articulated a simple vision—at least for her Plan A: "My vision is to travel, spend time with my grandchildren, and volunteer."

Take some time now or schedule some time on your calendar to write up your draft vision statement for your Next Chapter. This exercise is instrumental to creating the future you desire. We will ask you to refer back to your vision in Conversation 5—Course of Action.

OKAY, I HAVE A PRELIMINARY VISION—WHAT DO I DO NEXT?

Simply put, the remainder of this book addresses the question, "What do I do next?" As you develop your own vision, you will start to put more form around it, and you will begin to take action. In Conversation 4—Inspiration, you will share your vision and ideas with other people. In Conversation 5—Course of Action, you will build a plan for your Next Chapter.

Before you take too many steps forward, however, we suggest that you check in with yourself to clarify your level of commitment. The importance of commitment was strongly articulated in the book *Changing for Good*, written by James Prochaska and colleagues.[4] Through their research, Prochaska and his coauthors found that successful personal change is a six-step process. The first three steps involve preparation and commitment, whereas action does not occur until the fourth step. According to the authors, commitment "includes not only a willingness to act, but also a belief in your ability to change."[5]

Even if you are committed, don't be surprised if you feel some anxiety. The Next Chapter inevitably brings up emotions such as anxiety, worry, and fear. Prochaska and his coauthors offered some techniques that can counter the anxiety. For example, take small preparatory steps prior to major action, set a clear date to begin, and share your commitment with others. As Prochaska et al. wrote, "public commitments are more powerful than private pledges."[6]

In addition to committing to tangible, externally focused actions, you will also want to do some internal preparation. Internal preparation can help you enhance the critical mindsets and habits you will need for navigating your Next Chapter. It can also help you build your muscles of self-trust and self-confidence. Internal preparation may include the following:

- Trusting yourself to have the answers within

- Having the confidence to play big, even when you might want to play small
- Being willing to let go of former habits and activities that are no longer your top priorities
- Being willing to step into something new, ambiguous, and possibly unknown and uncomfortable
- Being willing to allow space and time, even a few minutes, for transition. Many people have likened this phase to the time and space between one trapeze and the next.

In summary, commitment is a deep, personal promise that you make first of all to yourself and then to others as well. It is a critical component of transitioning from a vision to action.

CONVERSATION STARTERS

- What lifestyle categories appeal to you, and why?
- How would you incorporate these categories into your vision for your Next Chapter?
- Are there any dreams that you've left behind and would like to add?

"You write your life story by the choices you make."

—Helen Mirren, actress

Inspiration: Select Your Traveling Companions

CHOICES

You just call on me brother, when you need a hand
We all need somebody to lean on
I just might have a problem that you'll understand
We all need somebody to lean on
Lean on me, when you're not strong
And I'll be your friend I'll help you carry on

—BILL WITHERS, "LEAN ON ME"

INSPIRATION

Opening Your Heart and Connecting With Your Supporters

When you think of the concept of inspiration, what comes up for you?

We believe that inspiration comes from many sources, including great books, movies, music, art, nature, other people, and spiritual leaders—in fact, any messages that touch us deeply. Inspiration may happen in a moment in time: for example, a child's pure joy, a pet's unconditional love, the birth of a baby, or a good laugh with friends. The list, of course, is endless.

Earlier in the book, we introduced our mantra: *Let go of your stories. Add your dreams. Keep exploring.* In Conversation 1—Culture and Conversation 2—Hurdles, you identified the stories that you want to let go. In Conversation 3—Options, you began to add your dreams by glimpsing a variety of lifestyle options and by creating a simple, preliminary vision for your Next Chapter. In Conversation 4—Inspiration, you will continue to add your dreams, primarily those related to your deepest feelings and your relationships with others.

Conversation 4—Inspiration is the time when you listen to your heart, allow yourself to be inspired, and connect with the people who are your loved ones and allies on this journey. Your allies represent your team of supporters as you move into your Next Chapter. They are the people who inspire you, and they will provide information or advice regarding how to navigate your choices. This conversation is also when you address the practical aspects of planning and holding important conversations with your team of allies.

This chapter presents three interconnected themes, plus we have interspersed research and examples of organizations that are demonstrating the power of our hearts and our connections. These themes are

- Opening your heart to the experience of inspiration
- Drawing on the people in your life
- Holding effective conversations about your plans for your Next Chapter.

OPENING YOUR HEART TO THE EXPERIENCE OF INSPIRATION

We have been particularly inspired over and over by the stories people shared with us as we were writing this book. One of our favorites is the story of Ruthy Friedman.

Ruthy Friedman, a dear friend of Gail's family, is a source of many levels of inspiration. As a Jewish child in Europe during World War II, she was given by her parents to a group of nuns and priests in Nice, France, to be kept safe while France was occupied by the Germans and their allies.

Ruthy vividly remembers being taught to walk in step under the nuns' habits, so that they could safely transport the children from one location to another while literally walking under the eyes of their occupiers. She also recalls having her name changed to Maria, having her Jewish star taken away, and hearing the "thump, thump, thump" of the German soldiers as they walked down a church aisle while looking closely at each child sitting with the nuns.

At the end of the war, Ruthy was reunited with her parents and siblings, and the family relocated to Israel. As an adult, Ruthy raised a family and held many jobs, beginning with serving in the Israeli Army as a secretary to Yitzhak Rabin. Now, at 82 years old, Ruthy regularly works three days a week as a volunteer at Baptist Hospital in Miami.

We are inspired by Ruthy's vitality, courage, love for people, and openness to life, especially given the tremendous challenges she faced as a child during World War II. In her retirement years, Ruthy is an Altruist, lighting the way for the rest of us to stay engaged and inspired.

Many people believe that inspiration simply comes to us at certain times and that it isn't something that we plan out in a systematic way or that we "make happen." True, the arrival of inspiration can't be controlled. We can, however, allow ourselves to be open to its arrival and even start to seek inspiration by doing more of the things that we notice can light a spark for us. For some that involves listening to music or going for a walk in nature; for others it is calling a good friend or visiting a museum.

A good place to begin is to notice what is inspiring you at this stage of your life. Perhaps it's a true story that you hear on television or the radio. Maybe it's a song or video clip that moves you when it plays, or maybe you see a couple walking down the street sweetly holding hands. Notice how that inspiration feels in your body, and allow it to be there without clear definition or form and without knowing where it will lead you.

When we think of inspiration, we are reminded of the following quote by Antoine de Saint-Exupéry, author of the classic children's story *The Little Prince*: "And now here is my secret, a very simple secret: It is only with the heart that one can see rightly; what is essential is invisible to the eye."[1] Like the essential things of which Saint-Exupéry speaks, inspiration is not something that can be seen but something that is instead felt by the heart.

Sometimes inspiration occurs when, as the old saying goes, "we stop and smell the roses." At those times, we realize that it's often the small moments in time that make a difference. Marilyn vividly remembers a time when she and her husband were caught in a snowstorm driving from Boston to Vermont. They were forced to stop at a lovely country inn, where they ended up having a delightful dinner together in front of a roaring fire. Gail often feels inspired at family meals—as long as she takes the time to pause and enjoy the simple pleasure of being together with those she loves.

On a recent *Today Show* episode, Hoda Kotb was interviewing Sandra Bullock. Bullock discussed motherhood, adoption, and the risk of staying in a "box" made from society's expectations.[2] She stated, "There are hundreds of thousands of children that are ready to be your child. You're a forever parent the minute you accept the love of that child. And it's amazing to me how we can take away people's happiness by telling them that this is the box you have to stay in. There is no box." Kotb added that she had been inspired by Bullock to adopt a child: "You never know who you might inspire."

In all that you contemplate and create for your Next Chapter, we encourage you to set a mood that is open to inspiration. Throughout this conversation and beyond, periodically check in with your heart. Is your current experience connected to what you love to do and what brings meaning to your life? Do you surround yourself with people you enjoy and care about? Do you feel inspired?

Research: HeartMath

The work of HeartMath Institute can help us set a mood that is open to inspiration. As it turns out, the heart is, in many ways, more powerful than the brain. In fact, contrary to popular opinion, the heart sends more signals to the brain than the brain sends to the heart.

Founded by Doc Childre in 1991, HeartMath offers two robust websites—www.heartmath.org and www.heartmath.com.

Over the last 26 years, HeartMath Institute has conducted and assimilated a large body of research around the power of the heart for optimal health and well-being. On the basis of this research, scientists have developed a number of tools, including a simple bio-feedback device, to enhance what they refer to as heart coherence, "a highly beneficial physical and emotional state."[3]

Research results include links between heart coherence and

- Improved focus, sleep, and calmness
- Reduced anxiety, fatigue, and depression.[4]

HeartMath Institute's website emphasizes the importance of invoking and sustaining sincere appreciation to achieve coherence and also to boost your immune system: "The greater your capacity for sincere appreciation, the deeper the connection to your heart, where intuition and unlimited inspiration and possibilities reside."[5]

An excellent way to bring yourself to a state of appreciation, gratitude, and coherence is through deep, slow breathing and allowing yourself to feel a sense of ease or think of something for which you feel grateful. One exercise is called the Appreciation Tool,[6] and its simple process is as follows:

Step 1: Heart-Focused Breathing: "Focus your attention on your heart area, and breathe a little deeper than normal, in for five or six seconds and out for five or six seconds."

Step 2: Heart Focus: "Imagine breathing through your heart. Picture yourself slowly breathing in and out through your heart area."

Step 3: Heart Feeling: "Activate a positive feeling as you maintain your heart focus and breathing. Recall a time you felt good inside, and try to re-experience the feeling. Remember a special place or the love you feel for a close friend, relative, or treasured pet. The key is to focus on something you truly appreciate."

As it turns out, the heart is, in many ways, more powerful than the brain. In fact, contrary to popular opinion, the heart sends more signals to the brain than the brain sends to the heart.

DRAWING ON THE PEOPLE IN YOUR LIFE: YOUR TEAM OF ALLIES

When you are grounded in your heart, it is a good time to reach out to those you love and those who are—or will be—allies or partners on your journey. Your allies will be sources of inspiration as well as practical supporters on your journey.

As you begin to speak more about your desires and preliminary plans, you may want to rally the people who will help you clarify, crystallize, and implement your vision. They are not necessarily people who make you feel comfortable. They are people whom you trust to give you the best of their advice and what they have to offer.

Your allies are people whose very presence energizes you to be the best you can be. You get to choose your team of allies, so choose people who invigorate and inspire you. Your allies have different roles. Some are emotional supporters. Others support you mentally, physically, or spiritually. Some advise you about possible paths you could take or avoid. Each form of support is valuable.

Some people challenge you in ways that you might not appreciate in the moment, yet you grow from the experience. Stephen Cope, the author of *Soul Friends*, calls this latter type of person a "Noble Adversary," in contrast to a "Noble Ally," to whom many of us often reach out first.[7]

On the journey through your Next Chapter, you may need advice, feedback, challenge, and moral support. Your team of noble allies and noble adversaries can provide this kind of inspiration for you.

Your team members may include your spouse or partner, children, siblings, dear friends, work colleagues, mentors, coaches, therapists, physical trainers, spiritual leaders, experts in a certain field or hobby, and many others. Some might be individuals with whom you interact infrequently, yet they always help you to see things differently, arrive at a new awareness, or even simply appreciate the small things in life.

> **As you begin to speak more about your desires and preliminary plans, you may want to rally the people who will help you clarify, crystallize, and implement your vision.**

Many individuals have built large networks throughout their lives, and they exemplify the two-way flow of giving and receiving. These individuals naturally turn to others for information, advice, support, and challenge, and they openly offer their support to others as well. The MetLife Mature Market Institute put it this way: "Invest in relationships. You need to plan ahead for the role your friends will play in your post-career life."[8]

Ronald C. Parker is an excellent example of someone who has been a lifelong networker and has a large team of allies. Ron spent the majority of his long career as an executive with a major beverage company, where he had numerous colleagues, mentors, and mentees. His allies have consistently been major sources of information, advice, and support. Likewise, he has done the same for them. At one point, Ron experienced a personal insight, and he realized that his role as a mentor was particularly critical for him. As he said, "My journey is not about me. It's about the next generation of leaders I impact."

As Ron approached his Next Chapter, he began to reach out even more extensively to many trusted advisors, friends, and family members.

He also spent time in internal reflection—conversations with himself—
to gain insight about his next step. As a result, upon retirement from
the beverage organization, Ron accepted a role as president and CEO
of the Executive Leadership Council, a Washington, DC, global nonprofit dedicated to the development of global Black leaders, a cause he
is passionate about.

After a few years heading the Executive Leadership Council, Ron
decided to retire for the second time. Again, he reached out to his
allies for ideas, advice, and information. He now says about himself, "I
flunked retirement twice."

We might add that Ron is definitely a Retirement Rebel. He has been
a Boomeranger, now he is an Altruist, and he is not done! He remains
very active in the Dallas community, and he continues to impact many
people in meaningful ways. As Ron stated, "My true net worth is my
network. What I mean regarding this statement is my personal and
professional value has been enhanced by the collective wisdom I am
able to access through these valued relationships."

Whether you are a Traditionalist who is fully "living the life"; you
are reinventing a new work world; or you are engaging in a combination of lifestyle choices, like Ron Parker, your team is important. You
might not explicitly use the word *team* to describe your allies, supporters, and advisors, and you might never convene them together in
a meeting room as you would a board of directors. Nonetheless, they
represent your team. They are the people who have your back as you
navigate your Next Chapter.

Your Personal Sources of Joy

At this time, it is also particularly important to allow yourself the
pure pleasure of joyful moments with other people, simply because
those moments feed you, rather than because you feel you must obtain
a certain objective.

Mary Sue Seibold was initially forced into an early retirement when
Braniff International Airways, where she was a flight attendant, went

bankrupt. At that point, she and many of her colleagues formed a tightly connected group. Now, 36 years later, they continue to meet for an annual event as well as multiple other lunches, dinners, and parties. They have fun together, they support one another when times are tough, and they have become like a family.

At times, all you might want as you engage on this path is to be around those who give you joy—perhaps even take your mind off yourself and your projects. Grandchildren are a classic example. With four young grandchildren, Gail often says, "I need a grandchild fix."

Conversation 4—Inspiration reminds you to build and deepen relationships with those you love and to appreciate your time with them. Some allies will inspire you simply through their presence to be your best self!

Surrounding yourself with a good team also keeps you happy and healthy. Many researchers have pointed to data confirming the importance of social connections for quality of life, health, and longevity. Conversation 7—Self-Fulfillment and the final chapter, Lagniappe, explore this concept in more detail.

What About the People You Don't Want on Your Team?

Now is also the time to think carefully about the people who are making you feel uncomfortable. How might these people be serving you? For example, are they simply allies who are taking the role of devil's advocates? Are they noble adversaries who might be pushing you in ways that lead you to greater insights and growth? Or are they more like "psychic vampires" who are essentially sucking your energy out of you?

As we noted earlier, noble adversaries have their value. The challenge is to distinguish between the noble adversaries and the psychic vampires. Psychic vampires, even if well-meaning, may deflate you with useless questions and negative feedback. They may give bad advice or advice that is more about achieving their own agenda rather than supporting you. At this stage of life, you don't need to be dealing with unnecessary negativity, so recognize who the psychic vampires are in your life and, if possible, let them go!

Some people fall in between these extremes. We all have folks in our lives who are good people and whom we like, yet who de-energize us. While your ideas and plans are still in the formative stage, it isn't the time to reach out to these people in hope of receiving their support, ideas, or encouragement. Later, when your plans are clearer in your mind, you can decide how to communicate with them.

The following quote from Robert Sapolsky is applicable here: "People who do best are those who have become more selective about whom they affiliate with. They've gotten rid of acquaintances. You don't need a lot of friends; you just need a few good ones."[9]

This is a time to realize that people move in and out of your life. As Jose Luis Herrera, a Peruvian shaman, said in a program Gail attended, "All relationships have expiration dates. Sometimes those expiration dates are related to death. Sometimes they are earlier."

> "People who do best are those who have become more selective about whom they affiliate with. They've gotten rid of acquaintances. You don't need a lot of friends; you just need a few good ones."—Robert Sapolsky

How Do You Select Your Team Members?

In his book *Good to Great*, Jim Collins used the phrase "getting the right people on the bus" to describe the importance for organizational leaders to choose a strong team.[10] This same phrase applies to building your team of allies who will support and inspire you during your Next Chapter.

In order to get the right people on your bus, think about where you particularly need or want help. We suggest that you review the following list and identify two or three areas that best describe the kinds of support you want. For example, do you want team members who

- Provide specific expertise or information that you may need to pursue your vision
- Connect you to others
- Inspire you to act
- Offer creative perspectives and innovative ideas
- Brainstorm possibilities with you
- Test your ideas and options, perhaps even as a noble adversary
- Help you clarify, crystallize, and evolve your ideas
- Help you work through challenges
- Help you plan conversations with others
- Hold you accountable to your vision
- Help you feel good about yourself and your life
- Or something else

In addition to deciding the types of support you want, you will also want to consider a number of qualitative factors about the people you select to be on your bus. For example,

- Who will tell you the truth as they see it and still honor your point of view?
- Who will challenge your assumptions and stories that could be holding you back?
- Who gives you joy? Who makes you laugh?
- Who really understands the ins and outs of what you think you want to do next?
- Who can put his or her personal agenda aside for your benefit?
- Who can teach you something you want to learn?
- Who can coach you through the process?
- Who do you want to know better and perhaps build a friendship with?
- Who truly cares about you?

Consider your answers to these questions. How would you like to use these answers to shape the team of allies you develop for yourself in the Next Chapter?

HOLDING EFFECTIVE CONVERSATIONS ABOUT YOUR PLANS FOR THE NEXT CHAPTER

Now that you have identified the people who will be on your team, you can begin to think about the conversations you want to have with each of them. These conversations are important because you are about to enter into something new, and you want the conversations to be effective. As Henry Wadsworth Longfellow is often quoted as saying, "A single conversation across the table with a wise man is better than 10 years' mere study of books."

Your Next Chapter conversations may be different from the conversations you are used to having. They may require you to be vulnerable, take risks, and move out of your comfort zone. You might also be reaching out to experts who don't really know you and whose time is very limited. Nonetheless, your Next Chapter conversations will have a creative element—an aspect of bringing your vision to life.

These conversations are also often a chance for you to crystallize your vision for your Next Chapter by declaring it out loud. As we discussed in the "CHOICES Map" chapter, a declaration is defined as "speaking that brings something into existence."[11] For example, in Conversation 2—Hurdles, Marilyn made a declaration to her friends and family that she loves what she does and that she has given herself permission not to retire.

There are many advantages to declaring what you want out loud and testing your Next Chapter goals with people you trust. In conversation, you can explore questions like, "Are my goals realistic? How complex is the learning process? Who else could provide information that might be helpful to me?" In some cases, you might ask for even more direct advice. For example, if the person knows you and the area you are interested in, you could ask, "Given what you know about me, how well would this lifestyle choice fit me?" Used in this way, conversations are the vehicles that move us forward.

You can speak your truth with confidence and total embodiment, or you can speak it with doubt. How you make the declaration may make all the difference in how others react to you and, in turn, whether they provide you with the support that you truly need. In Conversation 3— Options, when you created your vision, you were making a declaration to yourself. In Conversation 4—Inspiration, you are also making a declaration to your team.

As you prepare for each conversation, ask yourself the following questions:

- What support do I specifically want from this person?
- What benefits could this person receive from supporting me?
- How do I—or will I—support this person as well?
- Will we have a reasonably balanced flow of energy between giving and receiving?

This is not a "tit for tat" exercise. The flow of giving and receiving with another person might not be equal at any specific point in time, nor will the giving and receiving always be in the same currency. Often you might give through your time or your money. At other times you might give by making connections with others or by giving wise advice—the list goes on and on. The main idea is simply that a healthy relationship, even if it's strictly a business connection, involves mutual give and take. "How can I return the favor?" can be a useful question to build goodwill and open the door to creating the right balance.

What About Missing Conversations in the Next Chapter?

Exploring conversations a bit further, we observe the phenomenon of "missing conversations." These are conversations that perhaps you should be having but, for some reason, are not. Perhaps you hold back because the subject is touchy and you don't know how to begin. Perhaps you are fearful of the other person's reaction. Or perhaps you are so used to how things are that you don't recognize that a conversation might be missing.

In your Next Chapter, you may face even more reasons for missing conversations. Perhaps you don't reach out to a specific potential ally because your aspirations are still being formulated and you feel vulnerable about sharing them. Maybe you aren't confident that you have what it takes to achieve your aspirations, or perhaps you don't feel ready to handle the comments that might be made by a devil's advocate or noble adversary. The reasons go on and on.

It's important to recognize and give special thought to these missing conversations to be sure they are not preventing you from moving forward. Once you acknowledge them and the effect they have on you, you can decide the value of holding those conversations. If you feel that not having them is limiting you in some way, maybe it's time to explore why and commit to initiating them. This can be amazingly freeing, as it allows you to release the hold they have on you. In the next section we share some practices for holding these and other conversations that are important in your journey.

Practices for Holding Effective Conversations With Your Potential Team

As you are assembling your team, you may initiate many conversations with people who are currently or potentially on your team of allies. You might know these individuals well, or you might be meeting them for the first time. Below are some possible questions to ask yourself before, during, and after a conversation with a current or potential ally.

- **Plan ahead**

    o Why do I want to speak to this person? Specifically, what would I like from him or her (advice, connection to someone else, a job, etc.)?

- o How could I provide value to that person as well? What does he or she care about, and how does my request or project relate to that care?
- o What is the one most important outcome I would like to come from our conversation?
- o What help, if any, do I need from others to arrange this conversation?
- o Ideally, where or how would the conversation take place (office meeting, coffee shop, restaurant, phone call, video call, email exchange, LinkedIn conversation, etc.)?

- **Immediately before the conversation**

  - o What do I need to do to prepare myself so that I can approach this person with an open heart, a clear mind, and a mood of positivity and enthusiasm?

- **During the conversation**

  - o Am I staying present and engaged as much as possible so that I show up as my "best self?"
  - o Am I listening deeply, speaking clearly, and honoring the other person?
  - o What am I feeling? Am I triggered in any way? If so, how will I re-center?

- **After the conversation**

  - o What was the outcome, and what did I agree to do?
  - o What follow-up is needed (thank you note, email summary of outcomes and commitments, etc.)?

Barry McPherson's journey into his Next Chapter exemplifies the three interconnected themes of this chapter: opening to inspiration, drawing on a team of allies, and holding effective conversations.

A former high-tech executive, Barry is an example of someone who, during the course of his life, maintained long-time friendships and also fostered and cultivated a wide network of colleagues and trusted associates. Over many years and many situations, Barry's biggest inspiration came from his family and friends, who were always present and showed their unequivocal support. His wife, Sandra, who is retired from her own career with an aerospace corporation, has been an ongoing source of resilient dedication and support.

Several months before retirement, Barry began formulating the next phase of his life, and he reached out to a wide array of people—seeking ideas, counsel, and perspective. The best advice he received was, "Don't do anything" for at least six months or even a year. A close friend framed it this way: "You had a great run, worked hard, and did well. Now is the time to take a break, rest, restore, recharge, re-energize. Do all the other things you have been putting off for a lot longer than you may realize." (First on that list was Barry's goal to stop working three years prior!)

The same friend added, "Don't think of this change as retirement or not working but more as the next phase or journey of your life. You are not ending anything, you are just going in a new direction, one that does not have the overhang of all the burdens, challenges, and responsibilities that go with working in a high-tech environment."

Another friend amplified that advice by pointing out, "You are the way you are. If you start doing consulting only a few hours a week, before you know it you will be back at it full time. Why retire if you know you will end up doing that?"

After taking several months to consider the things that mattered to him for his Next Chapter, Barry framed out an exercise similar to the "sweet spot" exercise at the end of the Conversation 3—Options: *What are you good at? What are the things you like to do? Where and how do you want to spend your time?* Essentially, Barry identified his sweet spot. His focus (or vision) landed in three areas: People, Personal, and Passion. Most important to Barry was a desire to "give back."

From there, Barry reached out across his network. He was most interested in talking to people who had specific information and who could connect him to others, while leveraging new connections that arose out of those contacts.

Barry is now involved in multiple projects, and he continues to draw on others on a regular basis. His projects include coaching leaders in mid-career transition, consulting on operational excellence to a minor league baseball team, taking flying lessons, and investing in e-sports. In turn, he gives to others by sharing his insights and advice with his current and former colleagues.

Barry became involved in e-sports because he was introduced to a venture capital business that invests in sports-related start-ups. He capitalized on that introduction by engaging in an open, exploratory conversation with the founder of the business. As a result, Barry found a new interest. He now has an even wider network of people, and he is pursuing other opportunities in the investment and sports-related domains.

Most important, Barry has also found inspiration from the people and activities in his Next Chapter. He participated in a church-led mission trip to an orphanage in Costa Rica. When asked after a week of difficult physical work what part was the hardest, Barry responded that it was leaving the children behind. As he says, "I took this week to heart. I am inspired by what all these young ones have gone through and how they remain resilient, happy, and hopefully on the way to a better life."

> **"Don't think of this change as retirement or not working but more as the next phase or journey of your life. You are not ending anything, you are just going in a new direction."**

INSPIRATION AND TEAMS

As we were thinking about the concept of inspiration and the value of a team of people who are committed to a shared purpose, our thoughts went to *Captain Chesley Sullenberger*, who famously saved 155 lives by successfully landing a disabled jet plane on the Hudson River.[12] The following is a segment from the movie *Sully*.[13] This dialogue took place at the end of the National Transportation Safety Board's investigation.

Elizabeth Davis: "There is an x in this result. It is you, Captain Sullenberger. Take you out of the equation and the math just fails."

Captain Sullenberger: "I disagree. It wasn't just me. It was all of us: Jeff, Donna, Sheila, Doreen . . . the passengers, rescue workers . . . air traffic control, ferry boat crews, and scuba cops. We all did it. We survived."

While we certainly hope the unfolding of your Next Chapter will be less intense than the landing of a disabled jet plane, we think this image of a team is rather magical. You will be in the pilot's seat, and those whom you choose to support you could be helping you fly the plane, ensuring the safety of your ride, providing you with helpful information, or greeting you on landing.

CONVERSATION STARTERS

- Who are the people who have been the sources of greatest inspiration for you? Who have you inspired?
- What is your plan for reaching out to your potential team? Who will you talk to, and when?
- Which conversations will be relatively easy, and which ones will be difficult?

"I've learned that people will forget what you said, people will forget what you did, but people will never forget how you made them feel."

—Maya Angelou, author

Course of Action: Put the Pedal to the Metal

Alice: "Would you tell me, please, which way I ought to go from here?"

*The Cheshire Cat: "That depends a good
deal on where you want to get to."*

Alice: "I don't much care where."

The Cheshire Cat: "Then it doesn't much matter which way you go."

Alice: "So long as I get somewhere."

*The Cheshire Cat: "Oh, you're sure to do that,
if only you walk long enough."*

—LEWIS CARROLL, *ALICE IN WONDERLAND*

COURSE OF ACTION

Creating a Plan for Your Journey

One day, Gail and Marilyn were discussing what to cover in this conversation. "Hey Marilyn," Gail said, "we could put lots of ideas into this chapter—even the kitchen sink. What do you think are the most important concepts?"

"Well," Marilyn pondered, "I think a critical point is to write— not just think—the plan for the Next Chapter, and we have scientific evidence to back that idea up. What do you think?"

"I agree with you . . . yet lots of people will never commit their plans to writing. Have you done that?"

"Yes," said Marilyn, "I have a very simple plan. It helps me set priorities every day. How about you?"

"Well, I do believe in them, and I have written one." Gail thought for a moment. "Hmm. Where is it?"

"Maybe I should do the first draft of this chapter," Marilyn laughed. "Good idea."

We've shared numerous stories of how we, our friends, and our colleagues have stepped into or rebelled against traditional retirement. We hope these stories have opened up your mind and your heart to the myriad of options available to you as you contemplate the next step in your journey. We also hope that you have allowed yourself to dream a little and that you have already started to incorporate your dreams into your Next Chapter.

The phrase "Add your dreams" from our mantra is particularly relevant for Conversations 3, 4, and 5. In Conversation 3—Options, you dreamed about possible lifestyles, read about choices others have made, and made a preliminary decision.

Conversation 4—Inspiration and Conversation 5—Course of Action are highly interdependent, in that the actions they represent are not necessarily sequential. In fact, you might want to address these two conversations around the same time. A simple approach is to think about them as two sides of the same coin—heart-related actions and head-related actions. Both are important for achieving a complete and balanced Next Chapter.

Now is the time to give voice to your vision by creating your course of action—your plan for this journey. Your course of action is the plan you will make in order to help you successfully bring your Next Chapter to life. Your course of action is there to keep you on the road to your destination. It's the doing that turns your dreams into reality.

In our work as executive coaches, we both use a development process with our clients that's similar to the one explained in this chapter, and we have seen over and over again how the process plays out in real life. Grand visions and big goals get chunked down into actionable steps, and what initially seemed lofty or even overwhelming becomes doable. A cycle of momentum gets created in which people take one small step at a time, which leads to a sense of accomplishment, which leads to the desire to take another small step.

Since the steps have been plotted out in advance with this approach, people can almost go into automatic motion. Eventually, the vision will be realized. It's like the analogy of the snowball rolling down the hill. Once you get it started, it goes and goes and goes, gathering size and momentum.

Jim Collins referred to this phenomenon as the flywheel concept in his book *Good to Great*.[1] He wrote that great things are not accomplished in "one miracle moment." Rather, most achievements are similar to the process of giving a little bit of energy over and over to a giant flywheel—building momentum, turn upon turn, until the wheel begins to turn on its own.

We invite you to approach creating your roadmap with a sense of adventure and curiosity to see where that road will take you. One step at a time wins the race!

> **Your course of action is the plan you will make in order to help you successfully bring your Next Chapter to life.**

BEFORE YOU CREATE YOUR PLAN

Reflection

Before you start working on your course of action, take some time to have a conversation with yourself and get clear on the choices you want to make as you pursue your Next Chapter. You might want to refer to Conversation 3—Options. Or you might already have a set idea about how you want to spend your Next Chapter. You might even find that you need more time to contemplate your options or to try them on for size.

In his book *The Answer to How Is Yes*, Peter Block wrote, "Transformation comes more from pursuing profound questions than seeking practical answers."[2] So, in this process, we encourage you to take some time for self-reflection.

This is a time to "go slow to go fast." It's another opportunity to reflect on your childhood dreams as well as your current dreams.

Jan Sharry, a partner in a large law firm, is following a reflective process as she plans for her retirement. She describes her current thinking as follows: "As I approach retirement, I want to make sure that I am challenged, active, and interacting on a daily basis with other adults. I worry that I will be isolated from all the intellectual challenges and interactions I have had. Although I want to spend more time with my grandchildren, I really don't want that to be the cornerstone of my activities. Enjoy them—yes. But I will need time for thinking and analysis, along with making sure I demonstrate my individual growth by having measurable achievements."

Jan is a Retirement Rebel in her own right, not feeling the need to limit herself to traditional retirement roles and instead allowing herself to explore a wide range of options. Because she is engaging in reflection before jumping into her course of action, she will be able to detect the ways her own vision for retirement is unique and not culturally bound. She will then be ready to identify the important aspects of her course of action, such as people, location, career, and structure.

Other People

One of the first decisions you might make is whether you will be creating this plan primarily for yourself or for yourself and your spouse or significant other. Or you might want to factor in the wants and needs of children who are still living with you, elderly parents or others you have responsibility for, or grandchildren who might be an important part of your life. If you are including others, now is the time to decide whether you will create the plan with them or just consider their needs as you create your plan.

This time presents an opportunity for you to hold reflective conversations with your partner and other important people in your life so that you can incorporate their dreams into your plan as well. For example, if your spouse has always dreamed of retiring to Florida but you hate the heat and humidity, it will be important to approach this tough topic in a way that treats your spouse with respect and invites discovery of a mutual purpose you both can get behind.

A body of work known as "crucial conversations" highlights that when we come from a place of respect, people feel free to let their guard down.[3] So whether you and your spouse decide to move to Florida or come up with a different plan that is equally satisfying to both of you, respectful and effective conversations will get you there.

Bob Dunham, founder of the Institute for Generative Leadership, emphasizes that conversations enable people jointly to create a desired future state.[4] Good conversations begin with a shared purpose or care, and they produce commitment. Commitment, in turn, produces action, and action produces results. Results allow us to achieve our goals and fulfill our shared purpose. Dunham further reminds us that when life is chaotic and we feel overwhelmed, we can always have the next conversation, and that will move us forward.[5]

Location

Another decision might be where you want to live. You might have crossed the "freedom threshold" and are no longer constrained by having to live near your job, your children's schools, or your elderly parents, and you now have the freedom to live where you want. If you decide to move, you might already have a location in mind.

Alternatively, one of the first things you might want to do is to research the best place for you to spend your Next Chapter. There's a great quote from the short story "Ten Days in Whitehorse," by Maggie Dort: "I'm lonesome for things I've never had, places I've never been. I want to go home but I don't know where that is anymore."[6] This may be the time to find "home." You might want to make time for exploring some locations you've visited briefly or wanted to see but never had the opportunity.

As J. R. R. Tolkien famously said, "Not all those who wander are lost."[7] This may be your chance to wander—whether you are exploring where to make your new home or simply engaging in a lifestyle of more travel!

Your Career

Like the punk rock band The Clash, of the 1980s, you might be at a point where you are asking yourself, "Should I stay or should I go?"—not just about where you live but about where you work. As you approach your Next Chapter, you may be considering leaving a company or a job. This is a very important decision and not one to be taken lightly, as it can have a significant influence on whether you start your Next Chapter on the right foot. It is a very strategic decision, because once you tell a company that you're planning to retire, they are naturally going to start thinking about replacing you.

Several people we talked to mentioned that they left a job before they were ready. One individual, whom we will call *Mary*, became frustrated when the company she worked for kept promising her a promotion but not following through. Out of frustration, she gave them an ultimatum: "Promote me or I'll take early retirement." They didn't promote her, and she retired.

A thought on giving ultimatums: One definition of an ultimatum is "a final demand or statement of terms, the rejection of which will result in retaliation or a breakdown in relations."[8] Be ready to suffer the consequences, or else you are just making an idle threat. In Mary's case, the company called her bluff. A year later, she was still looking for ways to fill her days with purpose and social connections, because she had not really been ready to retire.

Conversely, *Linda Catt* gave her company a year's notice and offered to use that time to train other employees to take over her responsibilities. She had been so productive in her career that her work ultimately had to be divided among five people. In appreciation for the hard work she had put in, the company gave her a very large bonus, which more than covered a three-week trip to Europe for her and her husband.

You can create a transition strategy by exploring what alternatives are available to you and thinking creatively about how you'll take advantage of any opportunities and benefits that may come your way.

Creating a transition strategy will make the transition smoother for both you and the company. This is especially important if you want to work part time or do some consulting for the company. Thinking through all the possible alternatives that might come up will give you a head start on planning the conversations you'll have when you share your decision to leave or retire with the appropriate people.

Another factor to consider as you create your transition strategy is that your work might be an important part of your social life. We talked in Conversation 4—Inspiration about how important the social connection is to one's health and happiness. Some refer to it as the "new social security." In Conversation 7—Self-Fulfillment, we will address social connections in more detail. In fact, research shows that social connections can strengthen our immune system, speed our recovery from diseases, and possibly contribute to a longer life. In contrast, when social connection is missing, "it is a greater detriment to our health than obesity, smoking, and high blood pressure!"[9] You may want to consider how you'll fill that void if your work provides a substantial portion of your social connections.

Structure and Routine

For some, work provides a routine—a place to go every day with a set schedule. Retirement is a time of freedom. Ask yourself whether you can step into the mindset wherein freedom feels full of possibility, or whether you anticipate you will feel lost without the structure of work. If the latter, you can consider whether work is the structure you desire to keep—or perhaps you simply desire a Next Chapter filled with other kinds of structure, like volunteering or taking classes.

In Barry Schwartz's TED Talk based on his book *The Paradox of Choice*, he said,

> "Part of the downside of abundant choice is that each new option adds to the list of trade-offs, and trade-offs have psychological consequences. The necessity of making trade-offs alters how we feel

about the decisions we face; more important, it affects the level of satisfaction we experience from the decisions we ultimately make."[10]

He compared retirement to the stage in a marriage when the emotional high has worn off and reality sets in. People look forward to retirement, and once it really happens they can experience "loneliness, boredom, and feelings of uselessness and disillusionment."

In fact, research has shown that people fare better in retirement when they keep to a busy schedule with three to four regular activities and maintain their social connections.[11] These activities can include part-time work, volunteering, and exercising, for example.

WHEN EVERY DAY IS A SUNDAY . . .

As you experiment during your journey through the CHOICES Map, consider what kind of structure you would like to build into your day. Many of us are accustomed to working in corporations, hospitals, and other organizations in which our days are structured around specific activities, meetings, and job expectations. When we retire from our professions, it's easy to let the days evolve without much structure. While this is wonderful in many ways, we can also end up feeling that we are "floating" randomly and missing opportunities to contribute in meaningful ways.

When you experience this sense of "floating," one option is to create habits that help to structure your time, while perhaps allowing a bit more flexibility and ease than you had in earlier chapters of your life. Sometimes your choices might provide a natural structure for your time.

Retired from two nonprofit roles as director of development, *Sheryl Wylie* currently holds a volunteer position that is similar in many ways to a paid job. For the past seven years, she has served as the chair of a buying team for St. Michael's Woman's Exchange, an elegant 60-year-old store that carries a variety of gift items for women, men, children, and the home. Although she has quite a bit of flexibility regarding when she works, she has significant structure in other ways. For example, she is completely accountable for the results in her area of responsibility. Additionally, achieving those results typically involves working three or four days a week and five to six hours a day, depending on the season of the year.

The rewards of Sheryl's "job-like" service as an Altruist are many. As she says, "I am able to continue making a significant difference in people's lives. The money we make at the Exchange goes into grants that provide funds for nonprofits serving people in poverty. I'm around like-minded people; my brain is challenged, and I feel I'm doing something to help this world."

In other situations, you might want to create your own habits to help you structure your time. For example, Marilyn plans the structure of each week to allow time for her business, time for exercise, and time with her husband and friends. Many experts suggest that even when people are retired, it's good to go to bed and wake up at the same time every day.[12] Our habits help us to structure the day so that we can contribute, be fulfilled, and live with ease and joy.

MAPPING YOUR JOURNEY

Now it's time to map your own journey into this new territory of your Next Chapter. This is when you commit your thoughts and dreams to a plan that will guide you forward. If you have a plan thoroughly in your head and don't write it down, you might wander off of the plan without meaning to and lose your sense of direction.

In contrast, if you commit your plan to writing, you will be able to break it down into doable steps that you can schedule on your calendar, making sure things actually get done. The writing makes the plan real. It also brings your voice into the course of action; the mere process of writing is likely to open you up to new insights and help your ideas take shape and become clearer.

Writing down your plan is a powerful exercise, as writing stimulates a group of cells at the base of the brain that make up the reticular activating system.[13, 14] The reticular activating system is your brain's ignition switch; it filters everything that goes through your brain and gives importance to the things that you are actively focusing on at the moment. The physical act of writing brings those things to the forefront of the brain. Once you write down a plan, your brain starts working to bring it to fruition.

Visually, the course of action can take many forms. Some of you will approach it as a business plan, similar to ones you created in the past. Others of you will just jot a few bullet points on a sheet of paper.

You might choose to write Plans A, B, and C, as we mentioned in Conversation 3—Options. Or you might prefer to write separate financial, health, and lifestyle plans for how you'll live your life in your Next Chapter.

How you do it is up to you; this is your story, designed in your style. The form isn't important. The point is to take the commitment you made during Conversation 3—Options to another level of specificity. From this place, you will launch the action steps you write in your plan. (Note: You can call this anything you want: life plan, postretirement plan, development plan, Next Chapter plan, priorities, goals, commitments, promises, intentions, or whatever seems to fit for you—as long as you use terminology that generates a sense of commitment.)

WHAT WILL YOUR PLAN INCLUDE?

We put together a process for creating your course of action that you might find helpful. Your process might include some or all of the following steps shown in Figure 5.1:

FIGURE 5.1: SIX STEPS FOR CREATING YOUR COURSE OF ACTION

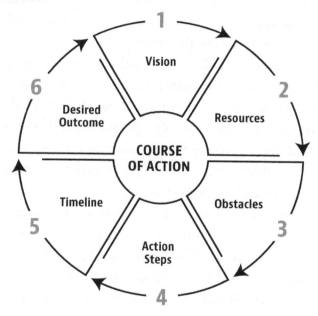

Step 1: Vision

Earlier in this chapter, we suggested that you take a fresh look at the vision statement you created in Conversation 3—Options and make any changes you want. Does it reflect you? If someone asks you what you're planning to do, does this vision incorporate your dreams and aspirations for your Next Chapter? These questions sound deceptively simple, but they are often the most difficult to answer. Allowing yourself to explore your deepest desires can be very frightening, but it's worth it.

It has been said that "a life of fulfillment does not usually happen by chance, but by design."[15] It may help to remember that you always have the right to revisit and revise your vision. You will probably find that your answers to these questions change over time and that the good life you've envisioned changes as well.

For instance, when *Becky Frank* retired, her vision was to travel, spend time with her grandchildren, and do some volunteering during her Next Chapter. After attending a presentation on how many homeless families there were in her community, she expanded her vision to include working with a core group of volunteers to start Family Promise of Grayson County to address this issue.

Becky has now realized that starting the nonprofit, in addition to other significant volunteer commitments, has taken more of her time than she planned to give to volunteering. She has decided to devote another year to getting the nonprofit operating and then to revisit her vision and find a way to bring balance back to her retirement. Becky confided that she thinks she really needs to create a new Next Chapter because she has spread herself too thin!

As you may recall, in our mantra, we added our dreams in Conversations 3, 4, and now 5. When preparing your course of action, this is still the time to allow yourself to dream, imagine, and create a mental picture of what your ideal life will look like for the next three to five years. As you do, consider all the important areas—in both your personal and your professional life.

If you already know what you want for your Next Chapter, you might have a very specific mental picture of what it is you will be doing, where you'll be doing it, and who you'll be doing it with. If you're trying different options on for size, you might imagine yourself living out two or three possible scenarios.

Once you feel comfortable with your vision and vision statement, you can begin to consider the resources you'll need to establish your Next Chapter.

Step 2: Resources

As you write down your course of action, include the resources you have available to bring your plan to life. What finances can you leverage? Who are your mentors and guides? Where will you get information to enact your plan? What kind of research will you do? Where will you do your research?

For example, maybe you are looking into doing consulting work after you leave your present job. You might want to talk to people who have already done this and ask them to share their experiences and any advice they have to offer. We both are often approached by people who want to start a coaching or consulting business, and we are happy to share our learning and experiences. Another option is to start by reading some applicable articles. If you search "how to start a consulting business" on Google, a large variety of articles comes up.

As you embark on your course of action, this is a time to consider your finances, too. Do you have the funds to do the things you want to do—to take that trip to Italy, buy that RV, or go back for a professional certificate or license? Can you afford to stop working? Can you cut back the hours you work, or are you dependent on a certain amount of earnings?

In her Next Chapter, *Darlene Elkins* decided to start a business selling her photography. When setting up her business, she wanted to create a website to showcase her work and accept orders and payments. Yet Darlene was on a fixed budget that did not have any room in it for marketing costs. At first she felt dispirited and worried she would not be able to hire a web designer. With some ingenuity, however, she came up with the resources she needed by bartering some of her photographs to a web designer she liked and taking a small loan from her retirement funds, which she will pay back once she starts selling her photographs.

In your efforts to find the resources you need to create your Next Chapter, you may naturally bump into some obstacles, as Darlene did.

The need for resources like money, time, and health can all come with their own set of challenges and trade-offs.

Step 3: Obstacles and Trade-Offs

Resources and obstacles are seemingly opposite yet connected concepts. Often, you might find that certain aspects, like money and health, can show up in both places.

The best way to manage obstacles is to anticipate them, so as you write down your course of action, ask yourself, What might get in the way? What obligations do you have? How can you manage them? A "can-do" attitude will help you to stay in a mindset of possibilities and to create a course of action with a strong chance of success.

This part of your course of action may ultimately involve making some trade-offs. For example, Darlene might have decided she had to forgo her website until she sold a certain number of photos, or she could have designed her website herself with one of the user-friendly online tools out there, knowing that it would look less professional.

Time, not just money, can also be a resource and sometimes an obstacle. We have both found this to be true in our own lives. We both want to work fewer hours than we did in the past, and this has required us to be more selective about the work we accept. We have found it can be very difficult to pass up work we would love to do, but we recognize the importance of making trade-offs to have the lifestyles we desire. We have gotten better at saying no, but we are still works in progress.

Health might also be an obstacle. Do you have any health challenges that will keep you from living the Next Chapter you want? How will those challenges limit your choices? How can you open your mind to new ideas that will allow you to get the most out of your Next Chapter, in spite of any health issues?

Tom Ervolina was thrown into his Next Chapter when he was forced to retire early after a stroke and brain injury that severely reduced his eyesight and challenged his mobility. Instead of letting his new disabilities render him hopeless, Tom is busily embarking on the next phase of his life, with business plans to launch a consulting and innovation center. Although he has to use a brace and a cane to walk and can no longer drive, Tom is still using his brain power, his years of corporate experience, and his PhD in math to do work that fulfills him.

Several of the people we interviewed stressed how important it is to expect the unexpected. For example, some people mentioned that they left their jobs before they were really ready and missed the social connections and the reward of doing meaningful work. Marilyn's brother missed the routine of having a place to go every day and the responsibilities of a busy executive.

Marilyn heard one of the most poignant examples of experiencing the unexpected when she struck up a conversation with a gentleman seated next to her on a flight. He had just moved his wife into a memory care facility. He had invested well, and he and his wife had plans for a wonderful retirement full of family, friends, and travel. Instead, his days are spent visiting his wife and seeing that she is well taken care of. As he reminisced about their unfulfilled plans, the gentleman seemed wistful yet accepting.

Many people encounter obstacles they didn't plan to face, and we certainly don't want you to obsess over them. We do want to encourage you, though, to take a little time and space to consider unexpected possibilities so you can put yourself in the best possible position to address them. Stories like Darlene's and Tom's offer hope for all of us and remind us that there are many ways to be creative.

THE POWER OF CHOICES

A few years ago, we contracted with a market research firm to conduct extensive interviews and focus-group research on how key events in the lives of successful people contributed to their later success. We asked the interviewees, "What events or situations in your life most contributed to your success?"

Seven themes emerged as having a major impact on the participants' later success. Some of these themes are typically viewed as positive events, while others are typically viewed as negative events. As you will see, some of these could most certainly be considered obstacles. The themes included the following:

- Death of a family member
- Personal accident or major health issue
- Professional setback or failure
- Risky professional decision
- Professional decision for work–life balance
- Impact of mentors
- Major accomplishments.

Regardless of the theme, we found that success ultimately depended on how people handled the situations they faced, rather than the actual situations.

Many of our research participants experienced major challenges, and those challenges actually spurred them on to greater accomplishments. They chose to handle their situations in ways that enabled them to grow as human beings and professionals. The results of our research reinforced for us the importance of recognizing when a setback can become an opportunity.

Step 4: Action Steps

Now that you have solidified your vision and have identified your resources and any obstacles you might face, you can begin to create your action plan, including action steps. This is where the flywheel concept we mentioned earlier, of taking small steps to achieve a larger goal or goals, comes in.

We highly recommend reading the book *One Small Step Can Change Your Life*, by Robert Maurer, which builds on this same concept.[16] In this book, Maurer demonstrates the power of identifying small steps, and he shows how small steps bypass the amygdala, the part of the brain where the fight–flight reaction exists.

Small steps allow you to operate more from the prefrontal cortex, the area of your brain where you demonstrate judgment, strategic thinking, empathy, and connection. It is certainly easier to complete your course of action when you have the clarity of mind to think strategically rather than be overcome with adrenaline and fear.

Completing this step allows you to add substance to your vision by getting specific regarding the details of your vision and how you will accomplish it. What would you like your average day or week to look like in your next phase? What will you actually do to bring your vision to life?

For example, if your vision is to sail more often, you might list the number of days a year you will be sailing, where you will be sailing throughout the year, and what kind of boat you will be sailing. Once you have gotten clearer on these specifics, you can list action steps to bring them to life: for example, sell your old boat, take part of your inheritance from your parents to buy the new boat you desire, research places to dock along your desired journey, and check yearly weather patterns.

Action steps fill the gap between where you are now and where you want to be. You can make that gap feel crossable by selecting your first action step. Maybe the first step for you is thinking about what your daily practices will be to maintain your health, vitality, and positivity while you are taking the actions you've identified. Maybe it's reading an article or talking to one of your allies about what your dreams and aspirations are. Whatever that first step is, as Nike's logo statement encourages, "Just do it." Take that first step, and then identify the next and take it.

As you start to take action, be sure to incorporate play into your plan for your Next Chapter, too. To do so, you might first have to relearn how to play. The *Oxford English Dictionary* defines *play* as to "engage in activity for enjoyment and recreation rather than a serious or practical purpose."[17] The baby boomer generation is full of workaholics, and many of us have defined ourselves by how hard we work. You might have to give yourself the freedom to slow down—to stop and enjoy life. As George Bernard Shaw is believed to have said, "We don't stop playing because we grow old; we grow old because we stop playing!" If you find yourself getting anxious when you imagine taking time to play during your Next Chapter, remember this quote!

Step 5: Timeline

Now that you have your action steps, what are your target dates for implementing your plan? Plans that have goals with dates linked to them create a sense of urgency and require another level of commitment.

When you first retire, you may get a lot of requests to volunteer or babysit grandkids. If you have been in the workforce for years, you may want to take time to "find" yourself again before making any or many external time commitments. If you choose to jump in and then find yourself overextended, give yourself permission to evaluate and pull back.

Karren McClure knew she wanted to do volunteer work, but she took a year off after she retired from a career in banking and didn't make any volunteer commitments during that year. When the year was over, she started volunteering with the DFW Humane Society and thoroughly enjoys it.

Terri West found it beneficial to give herself time to step back somewhat and not make any new commitments immediately after she retired. Following a long career with a large technology company, she spent her first year of retirement in what she describes as "recovery." "After working long hours and traveling globally for many years, I didn't realize how tired I was."

Terri did, however, continue her current commitments as a member of the board of directors for five nonprofit organizations and also as the vice chairman and then, a year later, as chairman of her corporation's foundation board. She adds, "No matter how prepared you are, retirement can be more abrupt than you expect. I have redefined myself. I'm not doing typical things, and I'm having a blast. It's really important to have plans and something to do upon retirement. Purpose is important—just purpose with a few less work hours."

What timeline is right for you? Do you need a full hiatus, or would you prefer to jump into action right away? It's your Next Chapter, so enjoy the pleasure of having the option to take a scenic drive or hit the accelerator!

Step 6: Desired Outcomes

This is a final check on your plan so you can make tweaks and later assess whether you have actually accomplished it. If you are successful in this endeavor, what will that look like? What will you have achieved? How will you feel internally? How will you know you are "there"? At this point, take a minute to check in with yourself.

When you are done creating your course of action, we encourage you to "play" with your plan and to try new things. The worst that can happen is that you find out something really isn't for you. For example, Marilyn thought she might like to create kaleidoscopes as a hobby in her retirement. She went to the annual Nellie Bly Kaleidoscope Weekend held every year in Jerome, Arizona. Marilyn found creating kaleidoscopes was not for her—she didn't like using the soldering tool. However, she did realize that she likes collecting kaleidoscopes and returned with several beautiful ones to start her collection.

Once you have drafted a plan, leave it alone for a few days and then review it again. Step back and check in with yourself again. What does your gut tell you? Does this plan "feed" you physically, mentally, emotionally, and spiritually? Does it give voice to something important within you? Are you enthusiastic about it and energized by it? Are you ready to share your plan—or at least the ideas within it—with those closest to you? Does your plan reflect the balance you want in your life? At this point, take some time and check in with yourself.

Ask yourself not just how your head thinks about your plan but how your heart feels about it. A plan based only on logic and reason might look good on paper but leave you feeling overwhelmed or empty when you go to execute it. A plan that honors how you *feel* about things will be grounded in what you truly desire to create. No matter what your head thinks, if your heart doesn't agree, you may find yourself putting up unconscious obstacles to your dream Next Chapter.

You now have a map for the next stage of your life. This plan is an evergreen document that you can add to and refine on an ongoing basis. In fact, one of the supplemental steps in your action plan might be to revisit your plan on a monthly, quarterly, or yearly basis to track your progress and to modify it as needed.

We encourage you to begin taking the actions delineated in your plan. In the vernacular of the business world: Execute the plan! This can be a time of excitement and renewal. Creating and following your course of action for the Next Chapter can lead you to the good life with the right place, people, and purpose in your life. Enjoy!

> **Ask yourself not just how your head thinks about your plan but how your heart feels about it. A plan based only on logic and reason might look good on paper but leave you feeling overwhelmed or empty when you go to execute it.**

CONVERSATION STARTERS

Step back and check in:

- Is your plan realistic? Do you need to make any adjustments to increase your chances of success?
- Does your plan give voice to something important to you?
- Does your plan reflect the balance you want in life?

"Reduce your plan to writing. The moment you complete this, you will have definitely given concrete form to the intangible desire."

—Napoleon Hill, motivational writer

CONVERSATION 6

Experimentation: Head Out on the Open Road

I hope you never lose your sense of wonder
You get your fill to eat but always keep that hunger
May you never take one single breath for granted
God forbid love ever leave you empty handed
I hope you still feel small when you stand beside the ocean
Whenever one door closes I hope one more opens
Promise me that you'll give faith a fighting chance
And when you get the choice to sit it out or dance
I hope you dance
I hope you dance

—LEE ANN WOMACK, "I HOPE YOU DANCE"

EXPERIMENTATION

Staying Aware and Continuing to Learn

With Conversation 6—Experimentation, we now enter a phase of continued action. This conversation does not, however, represent action simply for the sake of staying busy. Rather, it is about actively moving through your Next Chapter with a mindset of experimentation, a thirst for learning, a mood of curiosity, and a willingness to open one more door.

We believe that experimentation is a fundamental aspect of our lives during the Next Chapter. To a certain degree, a mindset of experimentation helps us to remain flexible rather than rigid and to consistently be "on the ready" to take new and different actions. In Conversation 6, you will try out your course of action, testing to see whether it fulfills you as you hope it will. If it does not, you won't get stuck or depressed—not for too long, anyway—because you have a mindset that allows you to change course and keep experimenting until you find the right lifestyle for you.

During the Culture and Hurdles conversations of the CHOICES

Map, you focused on reflection and letting go of the stories that have held you back. During the next three conversations, you added your dreams as you made decisions and took action. In the Options conversation, you made choices about how you want to live during the next chapter of your life. Then, in the Inspiration and Course of Action conversations, you took initial actions by identifying and rallying your supporters and by creating and starting to implement an action plan.

"Keep exploring" summarizes the focus of Conversations 6 and 7. Although Conversation 6—Experimentation involves taking action on the plan that you created in the Course of Action conversation, it goes beyond that. As you execute your plan, you do so with mindfulness and awareness of your external and internal worlds. You also allow yourself to pivot, or to shift, your plan over time if your needs and desires change. Conversation 7—Self-Fulfillment will also involve a spirit of exploration as you move toward greater levels of self-fulfillment.

Experimentation involves intentionally initiating change, embracing new ideas, and trying new activities. Sometimes you might actively seek change, as you refine your path toward a joyful Next Chapter. At other times, you might respond with an experimental mindset to changes that occur "to" you. In either case, experimentation helps you to cultivate your resilience, so you are able to try something new, notice when it doesn't work, and try something else if desired or needed.

WHY IS EXPERIMENTATION IMPORTANT?

The short answer to this question is that experimentation allows you to nudge yourself out of your comfort zone and, by doing so, live life more fully than you would have if you had played it safe. Your course of action is a plan with boundaries, structure, and ideas. Experimentation helps you get the most out of your plan and to expand beyond it.

If you engage in experimentation with an open mind, you can be on the lookout for moments when you might want to adjust your course of action. There is no need to get everything right straight "out of the gate"—nor is that always possible. Conversation 6 gives you a cushion to explore, tweak, refine, and even reinvent where needed. It invites you to cultivate the attitude embodied in this quote attributed to Emerson: "All life is an experiment. The more experiments you make, the better."

Experimentation involves open-mindedness, curiosity, and a willingness to try something new. By experimenting, you open yourself up to the risk of failure, and you also open yourself to new possibilities and joyful experiences. In essence, you allow yourself to try different options and to determine which ones work and which ones don't. While you are experimenting, you can feel tremendous fear, great joy, and many emotions in between.

Experimentation requires a specific mindset that sees each step as progress when others see a setback or even failure. An attitude of experimentation allows you to be open to serendipity, surprises, and accidental discoveries. As Confucius said, "Our greatest glory is not in never falling but in rising every time we fall."

> **Experimentation allows you to nudge yourself out of your comfort zone and, by doing so, live life more fully than you would have if you had played it safe.**

Thomas Edison, the well-known inventor of the light bulb, embodied the spirit of experimentation. He was considered stupid by his teachers and fired from his first two jobs. During the process of invention, he tried numerous substances as the filament for the light bulb. Some sources claim that he made a thousand unsuccessful attempts, and many people would say that he failed a thousand times. When asked about this, Edison reputedly said, "No, I didn't fail a thousand times. The light bulb was an invention with a thousand steps."[1]

As Henry Ford said, "Failure is only the opportunity more intelligently to begin again. There is no disgrace in honest failure; there is disgrace in fearing to fail."[2] Just imagine what we all could create if we had that same mentality of experimentation and optimism.

In some situations, you might think that a particular choice of activity isn't ideal for your Next Chapter. Then you find that it turns into an incredible experience that somehow is right in ways you never could have logically predicted.

For example, *David Cummings* retired as a lieutenant colonel after 21 years in the Air Force. While in the Air Force, he acquired a master's degree in education, specializing in guidance and counseling. His intent was to be a high school counselor for his second career.

Once retired, however, David experimented. Over time, he realized that he enjoyed fishing, hunting, gardening, and doing projects around the house so much that he never found time to reenter the world of work. His interest in a second career diminished. Now a confirmed Traditionalist, David says, "Every day is a holiday, and there is no time for boredom."

In other situations, you might think that you have made the perfect lifestyle decision. You experiment, and then it doesn't pan out the way you expected. For example, we both have friends who relocated to be in the same community with their adult children and grandchildren, only to learn shortly thereafter that one of the adult children received a wonderful job offer in a different location.

Similarly, Marilyn and Brian have a number of friends who moved into their condo community when they retired. Although most of their neighbors love the condo lifestyle, with its myriad of activities and facilities, a few have found that condo life and close proximity to their neighbors is not as enjoyable as they thought it would be.

Of course, experimentation also has its humorous moments. For example, have you ever tried a new recipe for a dinner party that totally bombed? Both of us have experienced that. Inevitably, after a few moments of embarrassment and recommitment "not to quit our day jobs," we find ourselves laughing with our guests. Everyone starts telling stories about their own similar experiences, and we laugh harder with each story. Those are often the times we remember with great fondness.

For the remainder of this chapter, we will look at experimentation in more detail and focus on four interrelated aspects:

- Living with awareness and mindfulness
- Exploring with courage and resiliency
- Learning as a way of life
- Honoring your intuition.

Let's start with the first one.

LIVING WITH AWARENESS AND MINDFULNESS

When scientists experiment, they use the tool of observation to help them collect data. Conversation 6—Experimentation involves a similar kind of observation. Being aware—or mindful—of your internal world and of the external world around you is critical to navigating your Next Chapter. When you are mindful, you notice all aspects of yourself: your mental attitudes, your emotional equanimity, your physical vitality, and your spiritual connectedness. You also notice the people around you and the environments in which you operate. When you pay attention to how you feel on the inside and what you see and hear on the outside, you will start to gather the data you need to get clear on whether your course of action for the Next Chapter is actually working for you.

The concept of mindfulness has become increasingly mainstream over the past few decades. Jon Kabat-Zinn is the founder of the Mindfulness-Based Stress Reduction program at the University of Massachusetts and the author of *Wherever You Go, There You Are*. He defines mindfulness as "paying attention in a particular way: on purpose, in the present moment, and nonjudgmentally."[3]

Gary Gach has written a lovely book about mindfulness. It involves a simple mindfulness practice that is also the book's title: *Pause, Breathe, Smile*.[4]

The spiritual teacher Eckhart Tolle, author of *The Power of Now* and many other books, speaks of the Now—the present moment: "Nothing has happened in the past; it happened in the Now. Nothing will ever happen in the future; it will happen in the Now."[5] At times, Tolle really stretches our minds. For example, he challenges his readers with this advice: "Here is a new spiritual practice for you: don't take your thoughts too seriously."[6] Now that is food for thought!

For some of us, staying aware of the world around us is not easy. For example, Gail's family often calls her Admiral Oblivious because she can walk or drive by landmarks in a city without being aware of what she is passing. Recently, she was leaving a yoga class and chatting with a new friend. She had already put on her running shoes when she heard the instructor say, "Has anyone seen my shoes? They aren't in the cubby where I left them." Gail looked down at her feet and noticed that she had a comfortable yet unfamiliar pair of shoes on: the instructor's! Ironically, the yoga class itself was intended to enhance mindfulness.

In today's busy world, even in the potentially more relaxed Next Chapter, it can be easy for any of us to miss important landmarks and signals that are speaking to us. While you move through your Next Chapter, Conversation 6—Experimentation can serve as a reminder to cultivate mindfulness, which will help you to stay present and observant as often as possible.

EXPLORING WITH COURAGE AND RESILIENCY

What do we mean by exploring with courage? We are talking about taking risks, going someplace or doing something unknown and most likely scary. Exploration requires courage, bravery, and sometimes a bit of brashness. It also requires resiliency. If something doesn't work, how will you adjust to the situation? Will you view this as a failure or simply as a setback? It takes courage, too, to be resilient. Resilience is a choice—consciously or unconsciously—to get back up and try again . . . not to stay down or linger in a setback too long.

When we think of exploration, we often think of pioneers who are hacking their way through heavy forests, fording river rapids, or fighting off various wild animals. Or we might think of Sir Ernest Henry Shackleton, who explored Antarctica and is credited with saving the lives of his crew despite losing his ship, his sled dogs, and most of their provisions.

Many of us idealize explorers for their sense of adventure, their vision, and their willingness to step out of their comfort zone. Although it's great to admire others, it's also important to recognize the ways each of us plays the role of explorer at times in our own lives. You don't have to be "wild and crazy" unless you want to be; you can just be you, pushing yourself to explore in ways that fascinate you.

Although we often think of exploration in terms of territories external to us, sometimes our exploration involves our internal selves. For example, when you explore your old stories and beliefs, as you did in Conversation 2—Hurdles, you are often facing your internal fears and unknown emotional territory. Although you might have released many of your stories at that time, sometimes the old themes return, particularly as you experiment with your course of action.

> **Exploration requires courage, bravery, and sometimes a bit of brashness. It also requires resiliency.**

Creating Your Bucket List

When it comes to taking risks, whether they are internal or external, the label of "risk" can be highly personal. One person's risk may be another person's comfort zone, and vice versa.

As you experiment and explore in the Next Chapter, you may decide to create your personal "bucket list." Although each person's bucket list is different, the term generally relates to activities that we want to do before we "kick the bucket." Typically, the bucket list involves exploration of some sort and includes activities that were previously either beyond your personal comfort level or beyond your resources of time or money.

> The concept of the bucket list has become common language over the last few years and was exemplified in the 2007 movie *The Bucket List*.[7] In the movie, Jack Nicholson plays Edward Cole, and Morgan Freeman plays Carter Chambers. They meet in the hospital, where they learn that they are both facing terminal cancer. They decide to "escape" from the hospital, and they embark on a series of new and sometimes risky adventures, such as going sky diving, driving race cars, getting tattoos, seeing the pyramids in Egypt, and riding along the Great Wall of China on motorcycles.
>
> Step by step, Edward and Carter cross items off their bucket list. While doing so, they engage in these activities with a sense of humor and lightness. Although they know that they have a limited time to live, they are experiencing extraordinary aliveness and joy as they experiment and explore. One of our favorite moments in the movie occurs when Carter gives Edward an article about his favorite (very expensive) coffee, providing the two an unexpected chance to cross one more item off their bucket list.
>
> **Carter Chambers:** Read it.
>
> **Edward Cole:** [*reading*] Kopi Luwak is the world's most expensive coffee. Though for some, it falls under the category of "too good to be true." In the Sumatran village, where the beans are grown, lives a breed of wild tree cat. These cats eat the beans, digest them and then . . . defecate.
>
> [*pauses*]

Edward Cole: The villagers then collect and process the stools. It is the combination of the beans and the gastric juices of the tree cat that give Kopi Luwak . . .

[*Carter starts laughing*]

Edward Cole: . . . its unique flavor . . . and aroma. You're sh**ting me!

Carter Chambers: [*laughing*] Cats beat me to it!

Carter and Edward both laugh hysterically until they cry. Carter marks "to laugh until I cry" off the bucket list.

Most of us have less exotic items on our bucket lists than Carter and Edward (see text box). For many of us, that list involves travel of some sort—perhaps to specific countries or even to achieve a goal (such as to visit all 50 states in the United States). One of our friends plans to climb Mount Kilimanjaro with her daughter.

Gail and her husband, Jeff, have travelled with their bridge buddies to many locations around the world. They trade off decisions about their desired destinations on the basis of who has what on their bucket list. Over the last ten years, they have viewed multiple colonies of penguins in Antarctica, huddled in the original Ice Bar in Stockholm, enjoyed food in a Vietnamese home, swatted flies in western Australia, viewed a pride of lions in South Africa, camped in the Sahara Desert, and generally had lots of good wine, food, and laughs.

Others have different items on their bucket list. Marilyn and Brian's bucket list included having a home on a lake. Some contemporaries have a list of A-level golf courses they want to play. For others, the bucket list is simply relaxed time with friends and family.

When you explore with your own brand of courage and resilience, you will be free to map new territories in your life that address not only your bucket list but also your feeling of aliveness and well-being. The tagline for the *Star Trek* TV series and movies describes an extreme form of exploration remembered by many baby boomers: "to explore strange new worlds, to seek out new life and new civilizations, to boldly go where no one has gone before."

LEARNING AS A WAY OF LIFE

Another way of looking at experimentation is to think of it as the cultivation of an attitude of lifelong learning. When you learn, you expand—mentally, emotionally, and often spiritually. You become more than you were before. Often, you find that you also build an enhanced sense of self-confidence, and you look forward to the next opportunity to learn and grow.

Many experts cite Lifelong Learner as one of the most critical competencies that a person can have. It is certainly useful in the Next Chapter. Lifelong learning keeps us active, engaged, and challenged. It is good for our health and our overall outlook on life.

Karen Stuart embodies the meaning of Lifelong Learner. She retired early and has dedicated her time since then to experimentation and learning. Karen has delved deeply into numerous fields, including acting, improvisation, neuroscience, child development, poverty, and politics. At one point, she experimented with reading all the great classics. After a while, however, she decided that this wasn't energizing her, so she allowed herself to stop that learning path, and she moved on to another.

Karen highly values lifelong learning and experimentation. She explains her path like this: "I tackled a number of things without knowing how to go about them and not knowing whether I would be successful or whether they would be enjoyable and satisfying. Rather than being willing to fail, I think it is more about a willingness to take a chance and being okay if it doesn't meet expectations. As I think about it, no effort is a complete failure, because I no longer measure myself in terms of outcome but instead in terms of the quality of the experience for purposes such as advancing understanding or enjoyment. This type of approach to life, in my view, requires the willingness to take a chance on the 'new and different' as well as feeling okay if the effort doesn't work out as expected. Thus, it requires a comfort with the unknown and with uncertainty."

When it comes to the Experimentation conversation, Karen gets it. Her dedication to lifelong learning reminds us of this quote often attributed to Gandhi: "Live as if you were to die tomorrow. Learn as if you were to live forever."

> **Lifelong learning keeps us active, engaged, and challenged. It is good for our health and our overall outlook on life.**

Another lifelong learner is *Caroline (Carrie) Kienzle*. Carrie spent her career in education and librarianship. Ultimately, she became director of a large public school library program that twice was nationally recognized as best in the country. She served on several major American Library Association children's and young adults' award committees, including Caldecott and Newberry.

After retiring to Apalachicola, Florida, Carrie participated on various community boards and helped to grow the local library. In addition to furthering the education of others, she has remained open to her own continual learning. She continues to learn bridge and improve her skills by playing twice weekly, and she participates in two monthly book clubs. Oh yes, and she now has become a certified instructor in yoga and meditation.

Lifelong learning may have a positive effect on your health, as well. An article by John Coleman in the *Harvard Business Review* reported that "reading, even for short periods of time, can dramatically reduce your stress levels."[8] The article explained that "a recent report in Neurology noted that while cognitive activity can't change the biology of Alzheimer's, learning activities can help delay symptoms, preserving people's quality of life." An openness to lifelong learning not only gives you a chance to acquire new skills that will help you get the most out of your Next Chapter, it may also help you stay healthier.

HONORING YOUR INTUITION

Intuition has a lot to do with experimentation and learning. Why? At this point in your life, your intuition may be guiding you toward certain areas for experimentation. Your intuition also helps you assess which experiments are working for you and which ones are not. Being willing to trust and follow your intuition will play a major role in your ability to thrive during your Next Chapter.

Some of the typical external measurements of success—like promotions, professional acknowledgement, and earnings—are typically less available during the Next Chapter than before. Now more than ever, you will likely turn toward your spouse or your life partner, family, and good friends for advice and feedback. You probably also will naturally turn more inward to your own intuition to select your experiments and gauge their success or failure.

Intuition is a word that many of us throw around quite a bit. We might give advice like "Trust your instincts" or "Trust your gut," with the firm belief that we all have our own answers within. In fact, most experts say that we are all innately intuitive, even if we sometimes don't trust our intuition.

Have you ever found yourself thinking about someone and then, shortly thereafter, gotten a phone call from that person? That's a common example of intuition. Or perhaps you are interviewing candidates for a critical job. Although one candidate has exactly the right experience, for some reason you aren't comfortable with him. Your colleagues like him, and you don't know why you are wary, so you convince yourself that this person will do a great job. After all, he seems like a perfect fit, doesn't he? But almost inevitably, once he's hired, the person doesn't work out. That's the reminder to trust your gut!

When *Leita Hamill* retired after teaching English at a prep school for 30 years, she could have easily stayed longer. Her intuition, however, was speaking to her. "Retirement was definitely for me a matter of intuition. I was only 56 years old. It felt to me that I was at the top of my game, doing something I really loved, and that there were so many worlds outside of the world of academia that I knew nothing about. That need to keep growing is what nudged me and gave me the courage to leave my life's work of 30 years."

"Ironically," Leita told us, "I found that after retiring to learn something new, what I was sought out for was my knowledge of education. So I served on three boards: first, the boarding school where I taught; second, an experiential learning semester program; and, third, an organization dedicated to gaining access to independent schools for underserved students of promise. Fortunately, I had much to learn about the financial aspects of education, long-term strategic planning, public speaking, and fundraising in these roles. Therefore, my goal in retirement was met in an unexpected way."

Margery Miller has used her intuition throughout her life. During her full-time working career, she had many jobs, from Montessori teacher to CEO and owner of a manufacturer's sales agency, all the while doing business coaching, team building, and people development for other companies on the side. She taught many entrepreneurs how to work *on* their businesses, not *in* their businesses.

Now, in her Next Chapter, Margery continues working part time as an executive and personal life coach. She has always been passionate about mentoring women. That passion and her intuition led her to form the Great Girls Network, a movement through which diverse women of all ages help other women. Initially, she assembled large groups in a semi-annual gathering. As she did so, the participants found great value in the experience of meeting and networking with each other, so they asked for more.

Consequently, Margery organized smaller, more intimate Track meetings, that she called Growth, Transitions, and Be Well, and that gave participants a chance to work through various issues and further their individual growth. The Great Girls Network continues to add members, and there is no limit in sight. Margery's vision is that it will become an international movement.

Summing up the power of intuition in her life, Margery says, "Eighty percent of my decisions are based on intuition, and 20 percent are based on data. I fully listen to and respect my inner voice. I feel more confident being me than I ever did when I was younger."

You might be thinking, "How can I discern the difference between intuition and flaky ideas?" There is, of course, no magic answer. Probably the most important move is to get quiet, go within, and trust your inner self—and a higher power—for the answer.

In the book *Heart Intelligence*, Deborah Rozman, a leader at Heart-Math, provided the following insight into this question:

> The heart often whispers to us with quiet common sense. . . . The mind tends to rationalize our desires and reactions. . . . As you practice listening for the difference in tone, you may find that the mind and heart are like two different radio stations. When you tune to the heart station, your attitude shifts and you look for responses that are better suited for the wholeness of the situation. . . . The heart contains a higher intelligence software package, designed to provide the intuitive guidance needed for navigating life.[9]

We both believe that this advice from HeartMath has been helpful to us as we experiment, explore, and learn throughout our lives.

As you experiment, your heart may be the very thing that tells you, "This is working!" or, "This doesn't feel good!" Although your head may rationalize and tell you to stick with something well past its expiration date, your heart is there to help you cut to the truth. You simply need to listen for it.

CONVERSATION STARTERS

As you begin to put the ideas of Conversation 6—Experimentation into practice, we suggest that you think about your own definition of experimentation and the learning mindset that accompanies it. Consider the following questions, shared by Noel Hensley.

- What is it that interests you?
- What is it that provokes you?
- What don't you understand?

"It is not the strongest of
the species that survive,
nor the most intelligent,
but the one most
responsive to change."

—Attributed to
Charles Darwin

Self-Fulfillment: Find Your Yellow Brick Road

Thank you for the music, the songs I'm singing
Thanks for all the joy they're bringing
Who can live without it, I ask in all honesty
What would life be?
Without a song or a dance what are we?
So I say thank you for the music
For giving it to me.

—**ABBA,** *"THANK YOU FOR THE MUSIC"*

Self-Fulfillment

Connecting With Your Higher Purpose and Lightening Up

A s we enter Conversation 7, we focus on self-fulfillment. The conversations on Experimentation and Self-Fulfillment are very much about continual learning and exploration throughout your life. While experimentation has much to do with exploring the tangible aspects of your life, self-fulfillment is more about the intangible realms of meaning, peace, and joy.

The *Merriam-Webster Dictionary* defines *self-fulfillment* as "the feeling of being happy and satisfied because you are doing something that fully uses your abilities and talents."[1] Although we like the *Merriam-Webster* definition, in this book we also use *self-fulfillment* to reflect the ability to find meaning in your life and to live from your life purpose and your higher power. When you live in sync with your highest purpose, your life will reflect the best of who you are and the best of who you can be. Self-fulfillment is about being all you can be and about living up to your potential in life.

We also see self-fulfillment as an expression of one's spirituality, which tends to increase with age. In many ways, we hesitate to use the word *spirituality*. It is thrown about in so many contexts that its meaning is often unclear, sometimes misused, and frequently connected with specific religious teachings. Nonetheless, we use *spirituality* because we haven't found a better word to describe a concept that is inclusive of many different ways of thinking.

The *Oxford English Dictionary* defines *spiritual* as "relating to or affecting the human spirit or soul as opposed to material or physical things."[2] Think about this conversation as an opportunity to nurture the energetic part of yourself that can't be seen but exists nonetheless. We invite you to choose your own words and phrases to create meaning for yourself in relation to this conversation.

Conversation 7—Self-Fulfillment is a time to continue your exploration beyond yourself and your immediate world—to a sense of unity with all others and to a higher power or source. This conversation is more about your state of being than about what you actually do during the Next Chapter. It's about the bigger picture beyond you, including the legacy that you leave behind as a gift to others.

> When you live in sync with your highest purpose, your life will reflect the best of who you are and the best of who you can be.

FINDING JOY AND JUBILATION

Another lens for viewing and describing self-fulfillment is the state of joy. Self-fulfillment is less about achieving an end state of "perfection" and more about being present to the abundant joy that is all around you. It is about opening yourself to the beauty and pleasure in the everyday things you are surrounded with.

The song, "What a Wonderful World," conveys this mindset of appreciation and pleasure. To us, the lyrics of the song signal a profound sense of hope, joy, and aliveness. They also signify a celebration of the beauty in nature; a gratitude for the small things in everyday life; and a sense of inclusiveness for all, whether they be objects, plants, animals, or other people. We see Conversation 7 as a reminder of the simple joys of life.

Your joy in the Next Chapter can come from a variety of places—your grandchildren, extra time spent doing things you love, or a new vocation. It may come from reading more books, painting again, or taking your dog on longer walks. Joy may come from your sense of freedom. Latin American novelist Isabel Allende put it this way in a 2014 TED Talk:

> "What have I gained [in retirement]? Freedom. I don't have to prove anything anymore. I'm not stuck in the idea of who I was, who I want to be, or what other people expect me to be. . . . *Retirement* in Spanish is *jubilación*. Jubilation. Celebration. We have paid our dues. We have contributed to society. Now it's our time, and it's a great time. Unless you are ill or very poor, you have choices. I have chosen to stay passionate, engaged with an open heart. I am working on it every day. Want to join me?"[3]

Self-fulfillment involves celebration about where you have been and jubilation about where you are going. It represents a time to say yes to life.

It is likely that the decisions you are making at this time are more often for sheer pleasure and enjoyment than they used to be. The Next Chapter can be a wonderful time to rediscover the joys of who you truly are. In a sense, you can go back to the innocence of your childhood, now infused with the wisdom of your experience.

During this time of life, many people think about their power and purpose from a different point of view than they might have done in earlier years. In many ways, this is a kind of enlightenment—a "lightening up."

We think the value of joy is summed up well in a scene from *The Bucket List*, the movie we introduced in Conversation 6—Experimentation. In this scene, Carter Chambers (played by Morgan Freeman) refers to the two questions asked by the guards at the entrance to heaven.

"You know, the ancient Egyptians had a beautiful belief about death. When their souls got to the entrance to heaven, the guards asked two questions. Their answers determined whether they were able to enter or not. 'Have you found joy in your life?' 'Has your life brought joy to others?'"[4]

An answer of *yes* held the key to entry. In this story, joy is elevated to the sacred. Why not? When you are giving and receiving joy, you operate at an energy frequency that plugs you into the divine.

> **Self-fulfillment involves celebration about where you have been and jubilation about where you are going. It represents a time to say yes to life.**

HOW CAN YOU FOSTER YOUR SELF-FULFILLMENT?

We hope that you are as convinced as we are of the value of self-fulfillment. The question now is, How can you foster your own self-fulfillment? And how do you stay on that path when times get tough, your body aches, or you lose a loved one?

Conversation 7—Self-Fulfillment is a time to engage in practices—or ways of living—that foster joy, aliveness, and personal growth. We don't claim to be experts or gurus on the topic. In fact, we are beginners, and we continue to learn. Nonetheless, in this section, we offer a series of possible practices to help you cultivate self-fulfillment during your Next Chapter, what we might even call a mindset and a "heart-set" of serenity amidst the highs and lows of life.

Perhaps one or more of these will work for you, or perhaps you have your own practices that you already know bring you into a state of peace, appreciation, and joy as you go about your daily life. Either way, we invite you to enjoy this section and to commit to a small set of practices that work for you.

In the next few pages, we review five types of practices that can help foster your sense of self-fulfillment:

- Community and social connection
- Exercise and movement
- Meditation and other stillness practices
- Rituals
- Play and laughter.

This list is not comprehensive. It is simply a beginning, and we haven't tried to "boil the ocean" by including every wonderful practice or way of life that can enhance self-fulfillment, including critical health-related ones like sleep and nutrition.

Since there are many choices of possible practices, you have many options to choose from. Almost all of these practices have been written about and studied extensively, so you can find plenty of resources out there that present the "whys" and "how tos." Most importantly, remember this truism: The best practices for you are the ones that you will commit to and actually do.

COMMUNITY AND SOCIAL CONNECTION

More and more research is showing the importance of social connection as we age. Julianne Holt-Lundstad and her colleagues found that "having regularly scheduled social meet-ups gives people a sense of trust and security and is good for well-being." They advise people to aim for a variety of relationships. That way, "you'll get a wealth of different pathways to feeling connected."[5]

Dr. John Ratey, a contributor to the docuseries, *Broken Brain*, adds,

"One of the big ways to keep people well, to keep people from using Medicare B, is being more social and staying more social. It's even three times more important than if you exercise every day, which I think is one of the most important things you can do, which is twice as important as taking medicine as your doctor prescribed."[6]

In Marilyn's condo complex, people meet regularly to walk together, play cards or dominoes, or celebrate holidays such as Christmas and the Fourth of July. This leads to the formation of lasting friendships. Marilyn became friends with Sue Romanowski, a neighbor in her condo complex. They first started walking together, and then their connection evolved into social activities and ultimately into a close friendship. Even after Sue moved out of the complex, they have remained close friends and continue to meet regularly for walks, wine, movies, and lots of conversation and laughter, as well as emotional support when they need it.

As we mentioned in Conversation 5—Course of Action, people's daily schedules often shift when they retire, and you might want to plan intentionally for continued connection, whether that be with current friends and family, with new friends, or through new activities. Some people are active in their church, synagogue, mosque, or other religious venue. This can be a valuable way to stay connected to your core beliefs, continue to grow spiritually, live a good life, and maintain a sense of community. Other people find connection by taking a class on one of their interests, such as cooking, photography, or a foreign language, or by joining groups dedicated to specific activities, such as yoga, biking, or gardening.

It may take time to make new friends that fit with your new lifestyle. We encourage you to give yourself the space to do so at your own pace. If you are shy, go slowly and keep showing up. Consistency pays dividends, and good friendships can take time to develop. If you are an extrovert, jump in and have some fun!

Rich Fedock, Curt FitzGerald, and *Ed Galante* are former work colleagues who have found a rewarding way to stay connected. Now that they are retired after spending their careers in a global oil and gas corporation, they participate in a book club with other former colleagues. They describe their book club as follows: "We spend some of our time reading and discussing history books or biographies, some of our time reading the occasional adventure or spy novel, and the rest of the time just enjoying one another's company." In case you are assuming that these men are relaxed retirees, think again. Each of them continues to contribute significant personal time to the Dallas community and beyond.

EXERCISE AND MOVEMENT

It seems as if every day we see another piece of new research on the value of exercise and movement to our health, weight, memory retention, moods, relationships, and practically every other aspect of our life. So what produces all these benefits?

Research has shown that when people exercise, the increase in blood pressure activates the brain's fight-or-flight response. As a protection against stress, the brain then releases brain-derived neurotrophic factor, a protein that "has a protective and also reparative element to your memory neurons and acts as a reset switch."[7] That reset switch is the reason we tend to feel more relaxed and clearheaded after exercise.

During exercise, the brain is also releasing endorphins. These stressfighters "tend to minimize the discomfort of exercise, block the feeling of pain and are even associated with a feeling of euphoria."[8] This is often referred to as "runner's high," but it can come from any form of exercise or movement.

When you think about all the benefits of exercise—positive mood, a stronger body, weight control, and much more—you can see how this one practice can move you significantly forward in your path to self-fulfillment.

The beauty of exercise and movement is that you have many choices in this area, depending on your physical capabilities and predilections.

You could try walking (especially good for you if it's outside in nature), jogging, Tai Chi, yoga, Pilates, strength training, bicycling or spinning, swimming, aerobics classes, boxing, tennis, golf, basketball and other team sports, dancing, stretching … the list goes on and on. Researchers are also discovering that intervals of high and low intensity are health promoting in all athletic endeavors. Bottom line: the primary message sent by experts and researchers is, "MOVE!"

> During exercise, the brain is also releasing endorphins. These stress-fighters make exercise feel less painful and give us "runner's high."

MEDITATION AND OTHER STILLNESS PRACTICES

In Conversation 6—Experimentation, we reflected on the value of awareness and mindfulness. In the current conversation, we look at other practices to promote stillness, including meditation, centering, breath work, gratitude practices, and the Emotional Freedom Technique (otherwise known as tapping). These practices naturally cultivate the aspect of self-fulfillment that relates to *being* rather than *doing*.

Any form of stillness is good, and this is one of the most important daily practices that we can have. When you are still, you allow yourself to *be*, rather than staying on the *do* treadmill. These moments of stillness are good for your body, mind, heart, and spirit. They rejuvenate you and help you to live with joy, aliveness, and vitality.

Meditation

Over the last few years, the body of evidence supporting meditation and mindfulness has increased substantially, and researchers are initiating numerous new studies. In our research for this book, we found many different definitions of *meditation* versus *mindfulness*. For our purposes, we think of meditation as a stillness practice—ideally conducted on a daily basis—and mindfulness as an ongoing awareness of our internal and external worlds. Both are important in our everyday lives.

In his book *Secrets of Meditation*, Davidji shares an overview of multiple meditation methods, including guided meditation, sound meditation, visual meditation, loving kindness meditation, mantra meditation, chanting, and many more.[9] They are all effective. The key is to experiment so that you can find what works best for you.

Researchers are finding that a sustained practice of meditation or mindfulness can bring about major improvements in our physical, mental, emotional, and spiritual well-being. In his books, programs, and website (www.chopra.com), Deepak Chopra and the teachers at his Chopra Center have shared some of this extensive research.

For example, in an article for the Chopra Center, Sarah McKay describes research-based evidence for a wide range of meditation benefits, including more focused attention, increased relaxation, positive shifts in mood, enhanced self-awareness, improved health and well-being, reduced anxiety, reduced pain, and even structural improvements in the brain.[10]

In their book *Super Genes*, Deepak Chopra, MD, and Rudolph E. Tanzi, PhD, advocate for adopting meditation as a lifelong practice.[11] They believe meditation should be the heart of well-being and that it can be a pathway to achieving our goals and desires. Among other benefits, the authors highlight the impact of meditation on success, including emotional resiliency, the ability to make good decisions, the ability to focus and concentrate, strong coping skills in the face of high stress, and many more.

When we meditate, we move into the day feeling lighter, calmer, and more at peace. Our spirit is nurtured, and we reflect that inner peace out into the world.

If you haven't meditated before, don't be fooled by its seeming simplicity. Some forms of meditation simply ask you to observe your breath. Gail will verify that it isn't easy for her to just observe her breath, so she studied and became certified in a mantra-based meditation practice called Primordial Sound Meditation, taught at the Chopra Center. Also, although it's relatively easy for her to meditate first thing in the morning, it's much harder later in the day, when she is "revved up." At those times, any form of stillness or going within is tough for her—although very important.

Centering

Sometimes, the best thing you can do for yourself is take a minute or two during the day to center yourself. In their book *Retooling on the Run*, Stuart Heller and David Sheppard Surrenda discuss the practice of Centered Presence.

> "The basic concept behind Centered Presence is to expand the field of your attention to include your entire body. . . . To assist you in cultivating the practical experience of the whole body as the center, we have identified four key anchor points for your kinesthetic awareness (feet, hands, head, and breath)."[12]

Heller and Surrenda further emphasize that "presence is vital to power. People respond to your presence even more than they do to your message. . . . When you lose active awareness of any part of yourself, you sacrifice presence and diminish your capacity for action."[13]

Centering can be as simple as putting your feet on the ground and taking three deep breaths. Deepak Chopra recommends a simple process based on the acronym STOP:

> "Stop. Take three deep breaths and smile everywhere in your body, observing what's happening in your body. Proceed now with kindness and understanding."[14]

> **Sometimes, the best thing you can do for yourself is take a minute or two during the day to center yourself.**

Breath Work

Some people like to do breath work, often called *pranayama*. Breath is also a critical component of yoga practice. A good description of *pranayama* is

"the conscious and deliberate control and regulation of the breath (*Prana* means breath, *ayama* means to control, to regulate). With each breath we absorb not only oxygen, but also *Prana*. *Prana* is cosmic energy, the power in the Universe that creates, preserves and changes. It is the basic element of life and consciousness."[15]

There are many different forms of breath work. In *The Healing Self*, Deepak Chopra and Rudolph Tanzi recommend a mindful breathing technique, summarized as follows: Take deep, relaxed breaths. Inhale while counting to four, hold the breath for a moment, and then exhale while counting to six. Continue for a minimum of 10 breaths.[16]

Andrew Weil suggests a technique often called 4-7-8 breathing, summarized as follows:[17]

- Place the tip of your tongue against the ridge of your mouth, behind your upper teeth.
- Exhale completely through your mouth, making a *whoosh* sound.
- Inhale through your nose to a count of four.
- Hold your breath to a count of seven.
- Exhale through your mouth to a count of eight.
- Do four breaths two to four times a day.

Why do breath work? The deep breathing of *pranayama* works as a purification process for the body. It "enriches the blood with oxygen, sending large amounts of oxygen to the brain, heart, and capillaries."[18] In summary, it helps your body, mind, and spirit feel great!

Gratitude Practices

Another highly effective and simple exercise is maintaining a gratitude practice. This can take many forms. One simple approach is often done at bedtime, and it involves thinking about—and preferably writing down—three things that you are grateful for each day. It's particularly valuable if you allow your heart, mind, and body to feel that gratitude for a few minutes—to revel in it.

On especially difficult days, we like to remind ourselves of the following quote: "If you have nothing to be grateful for, check your pulse. Being alive to live another day is what we should always be grateful for."[19]

EMOTIONAL FREEDOM TECHNIQUE—TAPPING

The Emotional Freedom Technique (EFT), also known as tapping, is another methodology that is becoming increasingly popular, particularly to reduce stress, challenging emotions, and pain.[20] The science and body of research supporting the benefits of tapping are growing rapidly. This methodology combines ancient Chinese acupressure and modern Western psychology. Its primary function is to calm the amygdala, the part of the brain that signals the body to activate the fight-or-flight stress response.

Tapping was initially developed by Dr. Roger Callahan and then further refined and simplified by Gary Craig. Many experts, such as Dr. Dawson Church and Dr. David Feinstein, have continued to research and advocate tapping over the years. One of the most well-known advocates, Nick Ortner, author of *The Tapping Solution,* has been instrumental in taking tapping mainstream.[21] For example, he and his sister, Jessica Ortner, have produced the Tapping World Summit, a 10-day online experience, for the past 10 years.

Gail recently enrolled in a program called Simplified EFT, a process developed by Valerie Lis after many years of experience as a practitioner and teacher. This methodology is a promising innovation to the EFT body of work and delivers quick, efficient, and effective results.

We highly recommend tapping for a wide range of concerns, including stress, anxiety, pain, phobias, allergies, overwhelm, and fears of any sort. The technique involves gently tapping on the endpoints of your meridians while focusing on a body sensation or emotion. The protocol calms the fight-or-flight response, and it is simple, fast, and effective.

The core technique involves eight meridian points (eyebrow, side of eye, under eye, under nose, chin, collarbone, under arm, and top of head). Additionally, there are many variations to this technique, depending on the expert or school of thought. To learn more, you can watch videos on YouTube or visit websites such as www.thetappingsolution.com or http://simpleeft. com/Simple_EFT_Tapping_2_VKLP.html.

RITUALS

Rituals often allow us to enter a special world and rise above our ordinary selves. At these times, you might experience a mystical sense of wonder, connection, and spirituality. In a sense, you get out of your own way during rituals, and you become the highest expression of yourself. Often, you might find yourself feeling deep connections with other people or experiencing a flow of energy that seems to fill you. In Peruvian shamanism, rituals often evoke a higher level of energy than that which occurs in daily life.

> Rituals often allow us to enter a special world
> and rise above our ordinary selves.

Many holidays and religious ceremonies involve rituals, such as receiving blessed bread at a Christian church as a symbol of uniting with Jesus or stepping on a glass at a Jewish wedding and saying *mazel tov* to congratulate the newly married couple. Rituals are key parts of many celebrations, particularly when they recognize life transitions, such as weddings, birthdays, baptisms, first communions, bar and bat mitzvahs, quinceañeras, and retirement parties. At other times, such as with funerals, rituals provide opportunities to mark a transition or to say goodbye to those we love.

In Peruvian shamanism, a special ritual involves preparing an offering, called a *despacho*, and then burning or burying it. A tribe of indigenous people in south-central Peru "believe that everything in nature is animate and in the concept of ayni, or reciprocity." They show thanks for the gifts that nature gives them with the *despacho* ceremony. They prepare a prayer offering made of "sacred items wrapped in small pieces of paper, including candy, cookies, seeds, stones, plant material, llama fat, tiny squares of metallic paper, starfish arms, metal charms, and more." The bundles are meant "for both general and specific purposes, such as attracting love or prosperity or for healing."[22]

After the bundle is made, the individual chooses the method to offer it. He or she may burn it, bury it, let the wind take it away, or let the water take it. "Placing it in the earth can represent gestation, releasing it to the water can be purifying, and burning it can be transforming."[23]

In Western society today, such a ritual would be unusual. We share it with you as a way to explore other possibilities. Your own rituals may have a completely different flavor to them. It is not so much the content of the ritual that matters as the meaning that we give to the ritual. Does writing a letter to someone who has hurt you in the past and burning it have power? If you can visualize the sadness and anger leaving your body as the ritual unfolds, it certainly can.

Rituals don't need to be unusual or extraordinary; however, they often add purpose, meaning, and enjoyment to life. Here are a few examples:

- When we were traveling together in Tarpon Springs, Florida, we noticed a group of older men who appeared to have a daily ritual of gathering outside a particular Greek restaurant. They always seemed to be laughing and telling stories.
- A group of folks in Gail's neighborhood meet at the dog park every afternoon between 3:30 and 5:00, depending on the time of year. They share neighborhood information, watch their dogs play, and build connections with one another.
- Marilyn has a group of dear friends she calls her "sushi sisters"— Kathy Burke, Suzanne Maxwell, and Debbie Townsend. She meets with them on a regular basis to share sushi and lots of conversation and laughter.
- At a luncheon the day before one of Gail's daughters was married, the women passed a candle around the table, and as each person held the candle, she shared a special thought or piece of advice with the bride.

Then there are rituals around the major transition of death. When Gail's father was dying, the family gathered around his hospital bed. Each person said a few words to him, hoping—in fact, knowing—that he was hearing them despite his physical state of unconsciousness. Then his caregiver, Dicey, sang "Amazing Grace," one of his favorite songs. Although everyone was grieving, they also felt a bittersweet sense of joy as they wished him well on his journey.

In the spring of 2006, Dr. Tal Ben-Shahar taught what was to become one of the most popular courses in Harvard's history—PSY 1504: Positive Psychology, a class that taught students how to be happy.

Dr. Ben-Shahar shared eleven happiness tips with his students, and the eleventh was to create rituals. Dr. Ben-Shahar said that "the most creative individuals—whether artists, businesspeople, or parents—have rituals that they follow. Paradoxically, the routine frees them up to be creative and spontaneous."[24] Dr. Ben-Shahar has been keeping a gratitude journal since September 19, 1999, and every evening he makes a list of five things he feels grateful for in his journal.

Marilyn can attest to the power of this gratitude ritual, as she has used it to take her through some times when she felt like a bank where life was making withdrawals but not putting in any deposits. By focusing on the things she was grateful for, she was able to leave behind self-pity and return to her positive, better self.

In summary, rituals serve a variety of purposes. Many rituals provide social connections, some foster inspiration, some allow time for play, and others enable life transitions. All, in their own way, provide an opportunity to feel self-fulfillment.

PLAY AND LAUGHTER

A very important aspect of self-fulfillment is the concept of play. What do we mean by play? Play comes in many forms. We believe that play is different for each person, and it also differs by the circumstances one is in. Most of the time, play is accompanied by a mood of lightness, childlike innocence, humor, and a pure sense of joy. When you embrace this way of being, you feel that you are living your life to the fullest—you are self-fulfilled.

Play can also be a way to set a mood. Work is wonderful when you treat it seriously yet with a light touch and a mood of play. Often, play is just a moment in time. It is not necessarily planned or expected—it just happens spontaneously. That moment of play can't be explained or repeated, but it is usually oh so energizing and memorable!

When we play, we often laugh. When we laugh, we are often in a mood of play. Most of us can remember situations where we laughed with friends to the point that our stomachs ached and tears were rolling down our faces. For example, have you ever been in a conversation during which one person said something funny, then another person added to it, and before long, everyone was almost rolling on the floor with laughter? When you are in those conversations, it seems that with every comment, the situation gets funnier and funnier, and you are laughing so much that it hurts. Then, the next day, when you share the funny conversation with others, they stare at you as if you have two heads! A moment in time?

> **Often play is just a moment in time. It is not necessarily planned or expected—it just happens spontaneously.**

An Irish proverb states that "a good laugh and a long sleep are the best cures in the doctor's book." A research study from California's Loma Linda University seems to back up that age-old wisdom.[25] Study participants in their 60s and 70s were divided into two groups: One group sat quietly doing nothing, while the other group watched humorous videos. The researchers administered a memory test and took saliva samples to measure levels of the stress hormone cortisol.

The researchers found that the group who had watched funny videos "performed significantly better when it came to memory recall" and "showed considerably lower levels" of cortisol than the group who had sat silently doing nothing. Gurinder Bains, a coauthor of the study, offered the following advice: "Find what makes you laugh and include it in your daily routine. . . . This can translate into improvements in your quality of life: mind, body, and spirit."[26]

One study conducted at Vanderbilt University found that 10–15 minutes of laughter a day can burn up to 40 calories.[27] In addition, "a University of Maryland study found that a sense of humor can protect against heart disease."[28]

Your own definition of play might be different from another person's.

It might include more time for sports like tennis or perhaps games like Rummy Tiles or charades. Or it may include more classic kinds of play, such as time with your family and especially with children, who have a zest for life that many of us want to emulate—or actually remember from our own childhood. Gail loves asking her grandchildren, "Describe something funny that happened today." The conversation typically ends up with all of them laughing until their tummies hurt.

Marilyn and her husband play the card game hearts with their good friends *Deb and Don Teeples*. These get-togethers include lots of conversation, laughter, and good wine, along with Don's favorite, Jack Daniels.

Gail and her husband have played bridge with a group of four other couples for 20 years. "Are we very good bridge players? No way!" Gail laughs. "When we play bridge, we talk, we drink wine, we share our experiences, and we laugh. We have become a family that we have chosen along the way."

Through playing cards with good friends, both of us have experienced the impact of connection and laughter on our personal feelings of self-fulfillment. In what areas of life do you enjoy play?

> Ten to fifteen minutes of laughter a day can burn up to 40 calories and help protect against heart disease.

CHOOSING THE BEST PRACTICES FOR YOU

So, with all these options, what practice is the best for you? We leave it to you to contemplate, experiment, and decide. The only "right" practice is the one that works best for you.

Here are some examples that have worked for us. Every morning Marilyn does a 15-minute meditation and yoga routine facing the lake, a practice that leaves her with a feeling of peace and calm. Gail begins her day with a mantra-based meditation. She also either attends a yoga class or performs the five Tibetan rites, a series of yoga-related exercises that were reportedly practiced by Tibetan monks.[29] Both of us also like to incorporate a morning walk into our routine.

Additionally, before we begin work together, either writing this book or working together on other projects, we often do a tapping exercise developed by Dr. Dawson Church, author of multiple books, including *The Genie in Your Genes* and *Mind to Matter*.[30] This exercise, shared during the 2016 Tapping World Summit, helps us to access our creativity, intuition, and higher power, and it helps us to approach our work with ease and lightness.

Ann Bentley retired from a career that included teaching, consulting, corporate leadership, and then teaching again. Currently a resident of South Florida, she continues to do some coaching, and she spends quite a bit of time each day in personal reflection. Focusing inward allows her to stay centered and connected to her own spirit.

"I believe that each of us is responsible for our own daily reflective time," Ann told us. "We all have a part in shining a light where there is darkness within our own lives and beyond. Let your light shine. It will change you. It will also change the planet."

Ann said, "Retirement has not slowed me down; however, it has changed my focus and brought a richer connected energy to my spiritual, emotional, mental, and physical life. This, in turn, allows me to focus that energy on others. We each have our part to play. This is mine!"

EVOLUTION AND RENEWED INNOCENCE

Throughout our lives, we all continue to grow and evolve as human beings. As we realize that we have probably lived more years than we have left to live, we become more aware of our mortality. Our personal goal is not to let that sense of mortality lead us into a depressive state. Rather, we want to allow our mortality to open up more gratitude, more joy for the small moments, and more play.

As we navigate Conversation 7—Self-Fulfillment, we recognize that life involves uncertainty and the unknown. Although we might want to live our lives with a limited number of surprises, we recognize that we can't predict what will happen. Uncertainty and unexpected change provide an opportunity for us to appreciate the circumstances of our lives as much as possible. As Eckhart Tolle said, "When you become comfortable with uncertainty, infinite possibilities open up in your life."[31]

By the time each of us reaches our Next Chapter, we have all been tested in different ways, and we know that we will be tested again. In our own lives, we (Marilyn and Gail) were both tested by an experience with cancer. Through our illnesses, we each realized that, symbolically, our cancer experiences were messages to live our lives differently.

In her novel *Island Beneath the Sea*, Isabel Allende shares a mood of hope and power in the following statement: "We all have an unsuspected reserve of strength inside that emerges when life puts us to the test."[32]

> **Self-fulfillment is a life-long process, not an end state. We are always on a journey of personal growth and evolution.**

Gail also remembers studying the works of William Blake and hearing her professor talk about three evolutionary stages: innocence, experience, and renewed innocence. Renewed innocence is a stage of development in which a person has seen both the light and the dark sides of life and consciously chooses to live with a childlike innocence, tempered by the wisdom of experience.

We find the three stages of development, particularly the concept of renewed innocence, to be quite compelling. In his book *Second Innocence*, John Izzo explores what it takes to rediscover our innocence as we age.[33] He states,

"There are only two basic ways to approach life. . . . The way of innocence ushers us to joy and wonder, while the path of cynicism takes us away from the experience of being fully human. The path of innocence promotes renewal, while the path of cynicism slowly erodes our spirits."[34]

As you travel on your own journey through the Next Chapter, we hope that you may discover your own renewed innocence—a chance to experience life in all its brilliance, through the wondrous eyes that come from living each day with awareness and mindfulness.

A FINAL THOUGHT ABOUT SELF-FULFILLMENT

Many of us have worked so hard for so many years that we have lost ourselves in our work and in what we think we need to be for others. In your Next Chapter, you have the freedom to take the time to rediscover yourself and find joy in who you are and who you have become.

There is no end to our potential as human beings. As such, self-fulfillment is a life-long process, not an end state. We are always on a journey of personal growth and evolution. Although the path almost always involves awareness, curiosity, and effective daily practices, the results are worth the effort. They include a vital, healthy, and joyful Next Chapter filled with meaning and contribution.

Bob Dunham describes his Next Chapter as follows:

> "This is a time of exploration, of discovery, of learning and growth. . . . In the end, life is about taking care of what you care about. That's where value, satisfaction, and meaning come from. . . . This can be enhanced with the freedoms of our elder years .. . . I think the lesson of life is to listen to the whisperings of your soul. Give it voice."

Since self-fulfillment is the final conversation, you might assume that you have reached the end of the CHOICES Map. In one way of thinking, you have. In another way of thinking, however, Conversation 7—Self-Fulfillment is a beginning. Our lives change over time, and we experience many beginnings and many endings. As you move through the various phases of your Next Chapter, you might want to revisit part or all of the CHOICES Map to help you plan for—or adapt to—the changes in your external life and your internal needs.

As we complete the CHOICES Map, we are reminded about the power of our dreams. As Angeles Arrien wrote in *The Second Half of Life,*

> "We are all born with a great dream for our lives, a dream that may have been derailed along the way by family and career responsibilities or submerged by our own choices. In the second half of life, after your roots have gone deeply into the world, it is time to resurrect this dream."[35]

CONVERSATION STARTER: HONORABLE CLOSURE

Attachment to the old form doesn't allow what's new to spring to life.

– Angeles Arrien

For our final Conversation Starter, we present a ritual called Honorable Closure, which was used by indigenous people to mark endings. This ritual initially was shared by Angeles Arrien and is described in the works of her students.[36] Mary Corrigan writes that

> Honorable Closure allows us the time for reflection and integration before we rush into the next thing. It helps us name the threads that we want to pull through into the future and tie off what we are leaving behind. It creates the space for the old form to give birth to something new.[37]

We invite you to engage in this practice as you complete the last step of the CHOICES Map and prepare for the amazing Next Chapter that lies ahead. Ask yourself,

- What am I grateful for from the experience?
- Where was I positively affected?
- Where was I stretched or challenged?
- Is there anything I need to say or do to feel complete?

"As we grow old, the beauty steals inward."

-Ralph Waldo Emerson, American essayist, philosopher, and poet

Lagniappe: A Little Something for the Road Ahead

I see trees of green, red roses too
I see them bloom for me and you
And I think to myself what a wonderful world

I see skies of blue and clouds of white
The bright blessed day, the dark sacred night
And I think to myself what a wonderful world

—WRITTEN BY GEORGE WEISS
AND ROBERT THIELE,
"WHAT A WONDERFUL WORLD"

CHAPTER 8

Lagniappe: A Little Something Extra for the Road Ahead

It is our hope that your journey through the CHOICES Map has opened your eyes to the many choices you have available as you approach, enter, or recreate your Next Chapter. You now have a model and tools that you can use to navigate your way to a joyful and satisfying retirement—one that can be the best time of your life.

In this concluding chapter, we offer some of the fascinating and encouraging research on longevity, centenarians, and suggested lifestyle practices for living a long and healthy life. Since both of us have roots in Louisiana, we like to think of this additional chapter as a *lagniappe*, a Cajun term that means a "little something extra." In Louisiana, shop-keepers and street vendors often include a lagniappe in with a purchase, throwing in a little something extra for the customer. This chapter is the little something extra we are joyfully offering to you!

While writing this book, we decided to do an experiment with some of our friends and colleagues. We asked them a seemingly simple question, "How long do you want to live?" In doing this, we learned that most of them haven't necessarily thought about how long they want to live. For most of them, it's not about longevity—or having "the most candles on the cake"—but rather about being able to live life to its fullest . . . to maintain vitality.

As we conclude this book, we will explore the concepts of vitality as well as longevity. Our goal is to share some recent data around how to live longer in your Next Chapter and how to let those years be ones of quality and good health. This is our "little something extra" for you.

> It's not about longevity—or having "the most candles on the cake"—but rather about being able to live life to its fullest . . . to maintain vitality.

CONJURING UP VITALITY

What exactly is vitality, and how do we get it and keep it? Vitality is the energy and zest for life that allows us to live a life full of purpose and passion. It is that wonderful life force that allows us not only to survive but to thrive and to experience self-fulfillment. Or, as the Star Trek blessing goes, to "live long and prosper."

In Conversation 7—Self-Fulfillment, we introduced five practices as critical for self-fulfillment: community and social activities, exercise and movement, meditation and stillness, rituals, and play and laughter. These practices will also help you maintain a vital life.

Many other authors have offered their own suggestions for maintaining vitality. Patrick O'Neill, author of *The Only Certain Freedom*,[1] shares seven ways to keep the fire of vitality alive: through passion, pacing, generosity, creativity, fun, rest, and asking for help. He describes vitality as "the personal energy that allows us to be active and engaged" and views vitality as "a renewable resource."[2]

When you look at O'Neill's list, what is the hardest item for you to master? For both of us, the answer is the same—pacing! We both often find ourselves overcommitted to work, family, friends, volunteer work—and the list goes on and on! Life offers so many opportunities that we are often victims of what psychologists call the "shiny-object syndrome." (So named because it's the equivalent of a small child chasing after shiny objects.)

Another item that Marilyn finds hard is asking for help. This can leave her feeling burned out and angry, so she has learned to take a look at why she allows herself to get in this situation and be sure she is doing things from a place of passion or generosity, not obligation.

For some people, maintaining vitality becomes hard when they lose their sense of passion. As O'Neill explains, "Passion is ignited when we have the sense that we are pursuing something bigger than ourselves, something that makes a difference."[3]

When you move into your Next Chapter, it can be easy to experience a loss of passion because you no longer believe you have a purpose in your life. Reigniting passion can reignite your sense of vitality.

A classic example of someone who found her passion later in life is Anna Mary Robertson Moses, better known as *Grandma Moses*. Grandma Moses loved to draw when she was young, but her life on the farm didn't leave enough time for her to pursue it. She didn't start painting until she was 78.

Grandma Moses's late start didn't stop her from having success as a painter. Her paintings of rural life in New England are displayed in the collections of many museums, and she is one of the most famous American folk artists of the 20th century. Her painting *Sugaring Off* was sold for $1.2 million in 2006! In her autobiography, Grandma Moses wrote,

> "I look back on my life like a good day's work, it was done and I feel satisfied with it. I was happy and contented, I knew nothing better and made the best out of what life offered. And life is what we make it, always has been, always will be."[4]

Grandma Moses passed away in 1961 at the age of 101. If she could find her passion at 78, so can we! What have you always longed to do or even had an inkling of interest in? It's never too late to discover your passion and pursue it successfully. In this pursuit lies the potential for vitality.

Grandma Moses was amazing! Lest you think that she is a totally unique, one-of-a-kind person, we would like to share another example. *John Lazar* is also an extraordinary person who, at 71 years old, continues to grow personally and professionally every year. He describes his journey as follows.

MY NEXT CHAPTER: JOHN LAZAR

More than 15 years ago, it hit home that I had not saved sufficiently to provide for a retirement I might want. It took me an additional 10 years (I'm a slow learner) to make the daunting decision to change the ways I was thinking, working, saving, and planning for my future. I chose to design a future that would allow me to have a great life of full-throated, open-hearted expression. To realize this possibility, I would have to live out on the "skinny branches," a venue infrequently visited.

One piece of good news was, and is, that I love what I do. I have a company that enables individuals, teams, and organizations to clarify and elevate their games to deliver better, often transformational, results and that fosters workplaces that are good places to work. We do this by providing focused leadership/executive coaching and blended consulting solutions for small and large organizational clients. Not only do I love this but I have enrolled almost a dozen extraordinary coaches to work with me on a project that will begin to unfold this year. This opportunity actually has me planning to expand my practice and migrate it to a business.

My upward trajectory is taking other forms as well. I am now collaborating regularly. Although it takes more effort, the larger offer that can be made and the increased quality of product or service are well worth it. I have made co-presentations at national and international conferences, cowritten an article for an international economics journal, partnered with another company to provide leadership coaching services to augment their collaborative development service offering, and solicited a colleague to be an advisor for a book I will be writing on self-leadership.

I have also elevated my leadership game through the coaching I am doing with millennial managers in several companies; serving on the board of directors of a society that has been my professional home for the past 35 years; and participating in thoughtful dialogue about innovative ways to deliver economic development for communities, cities and regions. The latter is a new domain and discourse for my engagement.

On other, nonprofessional fronts, I am doing a great job of reconnecting with and supporting my brother and sister, making quality time to spend with friends, building fun travel into my business travel when possible, using a personal trainer to get more fit and vital, and dating again after many years of resigned avoidance.

It seems to me that my recent choices and professional expressions are intentional acts of legacy. I am looking to leave the world a better place, to leave the people I work with better enabled to learn how to learn and improve performance and satisfaction, and to do that together, collaboratively. This is purpose-driven work, satisfying work that allows me to impact larger societal concerns as well as my own.

LONGING FOR LONGEVITY?

While vitality is about living a life of high quality, longevity is about living longer. We agree with our friends that a high quality of life is important, but why not live longer while we are at it? If you are interested, like we are, in the habits of those who have lived a long life, this section is for you.

Fortunately, we don't have to be magicians or to go it alone in our search for longevity. We have a valuable resource to guide us in our journey to maintain our vitality *and* live longer—centenarians. A centenarian is someone who is 100 years old or more. According to a study by the Pew Research Center, "While centenarians make up a small share of the world's older population, their proportion is growing. In 1990 there were 2.9 centenarians for every 10,000 adults ages 65 and older around the world. That share grew to 7.4 by 2015 and is projected to rise to 23.6 by 2050."[5]

Also according to the researchers, the group of people ages 80 and older has grown more rapidly than those ages 65–79. Additionally, the United States has more centenarians than any other country in the world, closely followed by Japan and China. India and Italy, the next runners-up, trail somewhat behind.

Due to a number of factors, including poor data collection and reporting, accurate data on centenarians can be challenging to obtain. Having said that, centenarians are often considered to be the fastest growing age segment in the worldwide population. By 2050, the number of centenarians is projected to reach anywhere from 3.7 to 6 million worldwide and 600,000 in the U.S.[6]

What can we learn from those who have reached 100 and beyond? Numerous pieces of research pop up every day that tout the importance of practicing the things that centenarians do to achieve longevity and maintain their vitality. We looked at the research from the Blue Zones Project, the Human Longevity Project, and various other sources. First, let's take a look at the Blue Zones Project.

Centenarians are the fastest-growing segment of the U.S. population. Currently there are 75,000 centenarians in the United States, and by 2050 there are expected to be more than 600,000.

Blue Zones Project

In 2004 Dan Buettner partnered with National Geographic and the world's best longevity researchers to identify pockets around the world where people live measurably longer and better. They named these areas Blue Zones, and they found that in these areas people reach the age of 100 at rates 10 times greater than the national average in the United States. The Blue Zones are Okinawa, Japan; Sardinia, Italy; Nicoya, Costa Rica; Ikaria, Greece; and Loma Linda, California.

Buettner created the Power 9, nine principles by which the centenarians in the Blue Zones live.[7] They are as follows:

1. Move Naturally: Be active without having to think about it.
2. Purpose: Take time to see the big picture.
3. Down Shift: Take time to relieve stress.
4. Eighty Percent Rule: Painlessly cut calories by 20 percent.
5. Plant Slant: Avoid meat and processed foods.
6. Wine @ 5: Drink red wine (in moderation).
7. Belong: Participate in a spiritual community.
8. Loved Ones First: Make family a priority.
9. Right Tribe: Be surrounded by those who share Blue Zones values.

We have mentioned the importance of most of these practices as we journeyed through our CHOICES Map. Two that caught our attention and that we haven't explored yet are the 80 Percent Rule and Wine @ 5.

The 80 Percent Rule appeals to us because of its simplicity: People should stop eating when they are 80 percent full. To put this into practice, you can repeat the Okinawan saying, "*Hara hachi bu.*" This statement is a 2,500-year old Confucian mantra said before meals to remind Okinawans to stop eating when their stomachs are 80 percent full. The theory is that forgoing the remaining 20 percent of food can make the difference between gaining and losing weight.

This theory is similar to the practice of calorie restriction, which became popular in the 1930s after research showed that restricting mice's food intake by 40 percent increased their maximum life span by 30 percent to 40 percent.[8]

Similar tests have been done at the University of Wisconsin on rhesus monkeys, a species that shares 93 percent of its DNA with humans.[9] Twenty years later, only 13 percent of the monkeys in the calorie-restriction group had died of age-related causes. In 2014, an update from the University of Wisconsin showed that the percentage had stayed stable.

> **The 80 Percent Rule appeals to us because of its simplicity: People should stop eating when they are 80 percent full.**

Next, since we are both wine lovers, we found it interesting that people in all Blue Zones (except the Seventh-Day Adventists in Loma Linda) drink alcohol moderately and regularly. The Blue Zones guideline is to have one or two glasses of wine each day, with a preference for red wine, and to do so with friends and with food. "And no, you can't save up all week and have 14 drinks on Saturday," states Buettner.[10] For those who don't drink alcohol, take heart—the Adventists don't drink either, and they are in a Blue Zone with long life expectancies.

The Blue Zones website asserts that by adopting a Blue Zones lifestyle, the average person could increase his or her life expectancy by 10–12 years.[11] While the research is still evolving, there are numerous examples of people who have become healthier and whose life expectancy has increased in cities where the principles have been applied.

LIVING LONGER IN THE BLUE ZONES

The Blue Zones Project was kicked off in 2015. Through this project, Dan Buettner has started demonstration sites all over the United States and has helped implement healthier choices in restaurants, grocery stores, and schools. The project also includes purpose workshops for adults and young people and has identified improvements that can make neighborhoods more walkable and bike-friendly.

The largest Blue Zones Project demonstration site is in Fort Worth, Texas, right in our backyard. *Natural Awakenings Magazine* reported, "As the largest Blue Zones Project demonstration site in the country, Fort Worth is well on the road to better well-being."[12] The city is working to become a Blue Zones Community, with residents, companies, schools, faith-based organizations, and restaurants working together to lower obesity, smoking, and chronic diseases and to make Fort Worth a healthier place to live, work, and play.

Another example can be found in Albert Lea, Minnesota, where a Blue Zones Vitality Project was started in January 2009.[13] In total, 3,400 residents of all ages participated in the project. Project experts and city officials joined together to create community gardens and intergenerational "walking school buses" (parents, grandparents, and volunteers walk children to school as a group). A sidewalk loop was constructed around the town's lake to encourage residents to leave their cars at home.

A total of 786 residents signed a Vitality Pledge and took the online Vitality Compass test to gauge their biological age. When the project ended nine months later, the results of the Vitality Compass revealed that the projected average life expectancy of the 786 Vitality Pledge participants had risen 2.9 years. (To read more research and articles on ideas for making your community and yourself healthier and happier using Blue Zones principles, visit www.bluezones.com.)

Human Longevity Project

The *Human Longevity Project* is a documentary series filmed in nine countries on three continents to uncover the secrets of the longest lived and healthiest populations on Earth. The film series, which consists of interviews with more than 90 scientists, physicians, healers, health experts, and centenarians, explores the question of whether aging can be slowed or reversed and the role our genetic make-up plays in longevity.

Contrary to what many of us have always believed, the researchers in the project explain that longevity is primarily determined by our environment, lifestyle, thoughts, and feelings, not our gene pool. It seems that we might have a lot more control over the aging process than we sometimes think we do.

The researchers in the Human Longevity Project support the mitochondrial theory of aging—the theory that the health and function of our mitochondria are the main factors that determine our biological aging at the cellular level. Called the "powerhouses of the cell," the mitochondria are responsible for producing the energy that our body uses to keep going.[14] It is the mitochondria's job to turn sugars, fats and proteins into the energy that is used by our tissues and organs.

So, the more energy a tissue or organ needs, the more mitochondria are in its cells. "In fact, the heart is so energy-intensive that up to 40 percent of the space in its cells is taken up with mitochondrial power plants."[15]

TAKING CARE OF YOUR MITOCHONDRIA

Everyone over 40 suffers from mitochondria decline, when the body makes less energy and the mitochondria are damaged. It is obviously very important that we take care of our mitochondria, as an investment in our health, our energy, and our happiness.

Fortunately, there are a number of things we can do to take care of our mitochondria:[16]

- Include a wide variety of colorful fruits and vegetables in your diet (aim for six to nine cups a day).
- Eat plenty of fiber to help detoxify your cells.
- Eat organic food whenever possible.
- Try to fast for 12 hours in each 24-hour period, to give your mitochondria a chance to regenerate.
- Avoid using antibacterial products, and make sure your cleaning supplies and beauty products are free of chemicals and toxins.
- Exercise regularly, including both strength training and high-intensity interval training.
- Spend some time in the sunshine each day (but be careful not to burn!).
- Spend plenty of time with loved ones.
- Include time in each day for meditation, prayer, or quiet reflection.
- Live as simply and minimally as feels natural to you.

Other Sources of Information on Longevity and Vitality

Numerous other sources are reporting evidence relating to longevity and vitality. A few of these sources are various works from Mark Hyman, MD, Christiane Northrup, MD, and Arianna Huffington.

Mark Hyman is the medical director at Cleveland Clinic's Center for Functional Medicine. Functional medicine is a system that "seeks to identify and address the root causes of disease, and views the body as one integrated system, not a collection of independent organs divided up by medical specialties."[17] Dr. Hyman has written numerous books, including *The UltraMind Solution: Fix Your Broken Brain by Healing Your Body First*.[18] He has also hosted several podcast series, including Broken Brain and The Doctor's Farmacy (see https://drhyman.com/podcast/), both of which present a wide range of advice on nutrition and health matters relating to our entire selves—our bodies, thoughts, emotions, and spirits.

Christiane Northrup has dedicated most of her career to helping women live healthfully and thrive throughout their lives, and she is the author of numerous books, articles, and newsletters. In her book *Goddesses Never Age*, she states, "Taking all the right supplements and pills, or getting the right procedure done, isn't the prescription for anti-aging. Agelessness is all about vitality, the creative force that gives birth to new life."[19] You can find multiple resources on her website, https://www.drnorthrup.com.

Arianna Huffington, the cofounder of the Huffington Post Media Group, is another prolific author who has written about health and her own personal wake-up call. In her book *Thrive*, she identifies a "Third Metric for defining success . . . our well-being, our ability to draw upon our intuition and inner wisdom, our sense of wonder, and our capacity for compassion and giving."[20]

Thrive and some of Huffington's other writings present research and suggestions on a number of ideas, including some areas we haven't covered previously in this book. For example, she emphasizes the importance of getting enough sleep as well as the negative impact of sleep deprivation on our "mental performance."[21] In addition, Huffington stresses the downside of technology, particularly overconnectivity.

"Its siren call (or bleep, or blinking light) can crowd out the time and energy we have for real human connection. Worse, there is evidence that it can begin to actually rewire our brains to make us less adept at real human connection."[22]

We have both also found that subscriptions to magazines and newsletters can be an easy way to keep up with recent research on longevity and vitality. Some that we subscribe to include the following:

- *Prevention* magazine and its website (https://www.prevention.com)
- *Mayo Clinic Health Letter* (https://healthletter.mayoclinic.com)
- University of California's *Berkeley Wellness* newsletter (www.berkeleywellness.com)
- *Consumer Reports on Health* (www.cr.org/cronhealth)
- *Women's Health Letter* (https://www.womenshealthletter.com/#)
- Food Revolution Network's mailing list, by Ocean Robbins (www.foodrevolution.org)
- Newsmax Health News Service (www.newsmax.com/health/health-news/).

Overall, research studies and experts seem to point in similar directions when it comes to cultivating vitality and longevity. For example, common advice includes the following:

- Eat real food
- Spend time with others you care about
- Get sleep
- Move
- Be mindful.

Regardless of which techniques you choose, your life in the Next Chapter may be extended with simple life changes like stopping eating when you are 80 percent full and eating organic foods whenever possible.

Although the information about vitality and longevity wasn't new to Marilyn, it really hit home when she realized that her grandmother was an example of the effectiveness of this advice. She lived to be 97, and until she was 92, she kept a huge vegetable garden and worked in it almost every day. She made sure every meal she served had vegetables fresh from her garden, and she used very few processed foods. Her garden provided exercise and serenity, and it might even have been a form of meditation for her. Definitely "food" for thought.

As a result of her breast cancer experience, Gail had a personal insight that led her to make a number of changes in her daily life, particularly in her eating habits. She now eats mostly a Mediterranean-type diet, focuses on organic food when possible, avoids gluten, consults with nutritionists frequently, continues to work out, and practices meditation most days. She still, however, is looking for better ways to sleep regularly and maintain healthy stress levels. It's a work in progress!

We suggest that you pick one new habit that attracts you today, find someone to share your journey with, and go for it. As many of those we interviewed attested to us, it's not just about longevity but about feeling vital for the remainder of one's days on the planet. Even if one new habit simply brings more joy and well-being to your day, it's worth the effort.

PLAYING BIG

If you do live to 90 or 100 or even longer, how many years do you have ahead of you—15, 20, 30, 40, or more? We encourage you to think about what you can accomplish with those years. Do you want to "play big"?

When we set out to write this book, we felt we had something to say, something to share. It was scary, because we knew that once we put the book out there, we were opening ourselves up to scrutiny and possibly criticism from people who didn't share our opinions or ideas. However, we felt compelled to tell our story and offer what we have learned along the road to our Next Chapter—so we took a risk and began this new endeavor.

We both have been successful in our careers, but before writing this book we felt there was something more for us to accomplish, a legacy to be left. So we decided to play big, and to us that meant putting this book out into the world and allowing it to take on a life of its own.

What does playing big look like for you? Many people think of playing big as making a huge, observable impact on the world—and it can be. At the same time, playing big can be much smaller. It could mean you've made one other person in your life happy, or you've made life better for a child or saved an animal. It could mean that you've made peace with someone in your life or that you really listened to someone with a different point of view and tried to understand his or her perspective. What a tremendous difference any one of these actions could make in our world!

Playing big is about pushing yourself out of your comfort zone. As Maya Angelou said, "Success is loving life and daring to live it."

Maybe these words from a quote attributed to Emerson can guide you: "To leave the world a bit better, whether by a healthy child, a garden patch, or a redeemed social condition; to know that even one life has breathed easier because you have lived—that is to have succeeded."[23]

Most importantly, we invite you to allow your own truth to guide you. You know better than anyone else what it is that will feed you, inspire you, and satisfy you in the Next Chapter of your life. A world of possibility awaits, and we are cheering you on—not from the sidelines but from our own roadways, where we are continually forging our own Next Chapter. With the CHOICES Map in hand, you and all of us in this stage of life can choose our time and place to get started. The rest of our lives can begin . . . right now!

APPENDICES

APPENDICES

A Recap of the CHOICES Map

For your quick reference, here is a summary of the CHOICES Map.

THE CHOICES MAP EXPLORES...

- The *Culture* and accompanying beliefs about retirement and aging that you have inherited
- The *Hurdles* that you have faced by internalizing and believing some of your cultural stories
- The *Options* that you identify for your Next Chapter
- The *Inspiration* that you experience at this time of life and the people who inspire and help you as you begin to take action
- The *Course of Action* that you develop to guide you through your Next Chapter
- The *Experiments* that help you to learn every day
- The *Self-Fulfillment* that completes you as a human being.

The Six Categories of Retirement

 Traditionalist—The Traditionalist stops working and engages in a variety of nonpaid, mostly leisure activities.

 Altruist—The Altruist stops working and volunteers, as a board member or in other roles.

 Lifelong Learner—The Lifelong Learner stops working and pursues a nonpaid activity that requires significant practice or continued learning.

 Stair-Stepper—The Stair-Stepper continues to work in the same career, while gradually cutting back.

 Boomeranger—The Boomeranger takes a break and then returns to work.

 Reinventor—The Reinventor continues to work in a new career.

The Six Categories
of Retirement

APPENDIX C

East Meets West

By now, some of you may have recognized a similarity in our CHOICES Map to the seven energy centers—often known as chakras—in the body. Our short response is, "Yes—there is a connection." The seven chakras were, in fact, our model—or foundation—for the CHOICES Map.

The chakras represented a guide to us as we developed each conversation in the retirement journey. They also helped us step back and feel confident that, on balance, the CHOICES Map represents a holistic model that will help you ask yourself important questions and engage all aspects of your being—your mind, body, emotions, and spirit.

The Sanskrit word *chakra* is typically defined as a spinning wheel or disk of energy that runs along the human spine. When all seven energy centers are open, aligned, and balanced, you experience physical, mental, and emotional health. You radiate vitality, that critical yet sometimes elusive aspect of human well-being. When you have vitality, you can make choices that enable you to live a full and meaningful life.

The current understanding of the seven energy centers—chakras—has evolved from Eastern wisdom traditions, specifically the Indian texts called the *Vedas*, written between 1500 and 500 BC.[1] One major scholar, Anodea Judith, defines chakras as "organizational centers for the reception, assimilation, and transmission of life energy. They correspond to the major nerve ganglia branching out from the spinal column, as well as states of consciousness, patterns of behavior, even stages of human history."[2]

Below is a summary of the seven conversations in the CHOICES Map and the primary focus of each corresponding energy center. The chakra summary is derived from the work of Anodea Judith.[3]

Those of you who know the chakra system well will also see that we have taken a few liberties in the way we interpreted each step vis-à-vis the relevant chakra. On balance, however, you will see the connection between the CHOICES Map steps and the meaning of the chakras.

Conversation or Chakra	CHOICES Map	Central Issue of Each Chakra
1	Culture	Survival
2	Hurdles	Emotions, Sexuality
3	Options	Power, Will
4	Inspiration	Love, Relationships
5	Course of Action	Communication
6	Experimentation	Intuition, Imagination
7	Self-Fulfillment	Awareness

The connection between the CHOICES Map and the seven chakras may reassure you, as it did us, that the CHOICES Map is a holistic model that honors mind, body, and spirit.

Additionally, you may choose to go deeper and further leverage the connection between the CHOICES Map and the chakras in your own practices, whether through yoga, meditation, or something else related to Eastern philosophy. For example, as you move through each step of the CHOICES Map, you may choose to meditate on the related chakra. Perhaps you will discover some other ways to leverage the chakras while moving through the CHOICES Map. This can be another opportunity to explore, experiment, and have some fun.

The *Retirement Your Way* Playlist

This is a list of the songs and quotes that inspired us as we wrote *Retirement Your Way*. We hope you enjoy them and add some of your own as you make your journey into your Next Chapter.

Conversation 1—Culture : "The Times They Are a Changin'"
Written and Performed by Bob Dylan

Conversation 2—Hurdles: "Climb Ev'ry Mountain"
Music by Richard Rogers and Lyrics by Oscar Hammerstein

Conversation 3—Options: "I Can See Clearly Now"
Written and Performed by Johnny Nash

Conversation 4—Inspiration: "Lean on Me"
Written and Performed by Bill Withers

Conversation 5—Course of Action: Alice: "Would you tell me, please, which way I ought to go from here?"
The Cheshire Cat: "That depends a good deal on where you want to get to."

Alice: "I don't much care where."

The Cheshire Cat: "Then it doesn't much matter which way you go."

Alice: "So long as I get somewhere."

The Cheshire Cat: "Oh, you're sure to do that, if only you walk long enough."

—Lewis Carroll, *Alice in Wonderland*

Conversation 6—Experimentation: "I Hope You Dance"
Performed by Lee Ann Womack
Written by Mark D. Sanders and Tia Sillers

Conversation 7—Self-Fulfillment: "Thank You for the Music"
Written and Performed by ABBA

Lagniappe: A Little Something Extra for The Road Ahead: "What a Wonderful World"
Written by George Weiss and Robert Thiele

A Conversation With the Authors

As we neared completion of this book, we sat down together and reflected on our personal journeys. As we mentioned in earlier chapters, we were each coming to terms with our own aging, and we were making decisions about our Next Chapter. One of our goals in writing this book was to use the CHOICES Map as we worked through our own stories, concerns, ups, and downs. We'd like to share with you a recent conversation between us that reflects some of our personal experiences.

Gail: Marilyn, we have been reflecting on our Next Chapter and, specifically, on our journeys in writing this book. How has writing this book been of benefit to you?

Marilyn: I've been going through the process of deciding what I want for my Next Chapter. By writing this book, I've become clearer about where I want to be, although I am not finished yet! I also love the fact that it has deepened our friendship and we have been able to help each other keep going in times of overwhelm. Finally, I believe that we have something to say, and, through the book, we can give our readers tools to help them go beyond what they thought was possible for themselves. How about you?

Gail: I have felt similar benefits: the process of working through the CHOICES Map for myself, the sheer enjoyment of working together, and the opportunity to help others see new possibilities and choices that give them joy and fulfillment. I look at our contemporaries and I see incredible talent, vibrancy, and continued ability to contribute. I hope that we can help them and help ourselves at the same time. Personally, I'm at a crossroads again, and I may be ready to choose a different mix of options. I want more days when I don't feel that my plate is full of work, and yet I don't want to empty my plate. The challenge of finding that balance continues to be tough for me. How would you describe your journey so far?

Marilyn: When I think about my journey, I recall a night a couple of weeks ago. I had committed to an intense amount of work for a specific client, and, at the same time, we were in the midst of editing some chapters. I was getting to the point where if I had to work on a particular chapter one more minute, I thought I would scream. I felt like I was on a roller coaster, and I wondered why I was doing this. But then, by the next morning, I felt a change; it was as if my mind had answered the question during the night, and I could feel my passion for the book come back. I felt peaceful and hopeful. It was joyful. How about you?

Gail: For me, I love to start things, so in the beginning, our process with the book was great. I was on a high. We developed our topic and our model, and I really felt we had something unique to offer. I also enjoyed the initial writing—putting our ideas on paper. Then the doldrums arrived. The editing and the refinement of each chapter felt onerous to me. Like you, I was overcommitting in other areas, and that aggravated my overwhelm with the book. I didn't feel a sense of play and lightness, so I was living outside of what we were saying to our readers. I knew that, and I felt guilty. It was like trudging through mud or deep snow. Now, the end is in sight, and my mood is improving. I'm feeling a sense of play again. I love to start things; I love to complete things; I don't like the middle stage. That's a pattern for me.

Marilyn: One area I've been thinking about is what would we like our audience to take away from our book—what would we like them to feel. I would like them to be inspired, to be excited about what could be, and to have hope. I would like our readers to feel that we have given them some tools that will help them along the way. I would also like to encourage them to "play big," as they define big for themselves.

Gail: I love what you have said. Taking on this book was, in itself, an act of "playing big" for me. Several times, I found myself wanting to shrink into the "small" me. Then something would shift; I would literally stand up taller, and I would look forward to making an impact. In terms of impact, I hope our readers feel that they have choices in their lives and that those choices help them feel vital every day. I also hope that they—and we—approach each day with joy and an openness to personal growth even when our capabilities may start to diminish.

—Marilyn and Gail

ENDNOTES

INTRODUCTION

1. Richard B. Wagner, "Retirement Is the Wrong Word," *Financial Advisor*, August 1, 2006, https://www.fa-mag.com/news/retirement-is-the-wrong-word-1444.html

THE CHOICES MAP

1. Robert Dunham, "The Generative Foundations of Action in Organizations: Speaking and Listening," *International Journal of Coaching in Organizations* 7, no. 2 (2009): 48.

2. Fernando Flores, *Conversations for Action and Collected Essays: Instilling a Culture of Commitment in Working Relationships*, ed. Maria Letelier (self-published, 2013), ch. 1.

CONVERSATION 1

1. Mario Martinez, "The Cultural Portal Theory of Aging," Thrive Global, June 9, 2017, https://medium.com/thrive-global/the-cultural-portal-theory-of-aging-dfe696375ebf

2. Mario Martinez, "The Cultural Portal Theory of Aging."

3. Aris Teon, "Filial Piety in Chinese Culture," *Greater China Journal* [blog], March 14, 2016, https://china-journal.org/2016/03/14/filial-piety-in-chinese-culture/

4.   Thomas Dillon, "Hitting 60 in Japan Offers a Chance to Start Over, so Don't Waste Time Looking Back," *Japan Times*, December 17, 2014, https://www.japantimes.co.jp/community/2014/12/17/our-lives/hitting-60-japan-offers-chance-start-dont-waste-time-looking-back/#.W5f_lvYnbIU

        Mock Joya, *Japan and Things Japanese* (London: Kegan Paul, 2006).

5.   "A Brief History of Retirement: It's a Modern Idea," *Seattle Times*, December 31, 2013, https://www.seattletimes.com/nation-world/a-brief-history-of-retirement-its-a-modern-idea/

6.   Dora L. Costa, *The Evolution of Retirement: An American Economic History, 1880–1990* (Chicago: University of Chicago Press, 1998).

7.   Larry DeWitt, "The Development of Social Security in America," *Social Security Bulletin* 70, no. 3 (2010).

8.   "A Brief History of Retirement: It's a Modern Idea."

9.   Social Security Administration, "Pre-Social Security Period," https://www.ssa.gov/history/briefhistory3.html

10.   Pension Retirement, "History of Pensions: Why Were They Started?" http://pensionretirement.com/history-of-pensions-why-were-they-started/

11.   Sarah Laskow, "How Retirement Was Invented," *Atlantic Monthly*, October 24, 2014, https://www.theatlantic.com/business/archive/2014/10/how-retirement-was-invented/381802/

12.   Sarah Laskow, "How Retirement Was Invented."

13.   Sarah Laskow, "How Retirement Was Invented."

14.   Joanna Short, "The Economic History of Retirement in the United States," Economic History Association, https://eh.net/encyclopedia/economic-history-of-retirement-in-the-united-states/

15.   Jill Cornfield, "Bankrate Survey: 70% Will Work as Long as They Can," Bankrate, September 7, 2016, https://www.bankrate.com/finance/consumer-index/money-pulse-0916.aspx

16.   Joanna Short, "The Economic History of Retirement in the United States."

17.   Joanna Short, "The Economic History of Retirement in the United States."

18.   Bureau of Labor Statistics, "Current Labor Statistics," June 2008, https://www.bls.gov/opub/mlr/2008/06/cls0806.pdf

19.   Bob Buford, *Halftime: Changing Your Game Plan From Success to Significance* (New York: Harper Collins, 2011), 200.

20.   Richard J. Leider and David A. Shapiro, *Claiming Your Place at the Fire: Living the Second Half of Your Life on Purpose* (Oakland, CA: Berrett-Koehler, 2004).

21. Social Security Administration, "Benefits Planner: Life Expectancy," https://
     www.ssa.gov/planners/lifeexpectancy.html

22. Lynda Gratton and Andrew Scott, *The 100-Year Life: Living and Working in an
     Age of Longevity* (New York: Bloomsbury, 2016).

23. Lindsay M. Monte, *Household Economic Studies: Current Population Reports*
     (Washington, DC: U.S. Census Bureau, 2017), https://www.census.gov/
     content/dam/Census/library/publications/2017/demo/p70br-147.pdf

     Sharon Jayson, "More Grandparents Than Ever," *New York Times,* March
     7, 2017, https://www.nytimes.com/2017/03/20/health/grandparents-
     population-census.html

24. Lillian Carson, *The Essential Grandparent: A Guide to Making a Difference*
     (Deerfield Beach, FL: Health Communications, 1997).

25. "The Grandparent Boom!" *AARP Bulletin,* 2017, https://www.aarp.org/home-
     family/friends-family/info-2017/record-number-grandparents.html

26. Catherine Collinson, *Wishful Thinking or Within Reach? Three Generations
     Prepare for "Retirement"* (Los Angeles: Transamerica Center for Retirement
     Studies, 2017).

27. Jill Cornfield, "Bankrate Survey: 70% Will Work as Long as They Can,"
     Bankrate, September 7, 2016, https://www.bankrate.com/finance/consumer-
     index/money-pulse-0916.aspx

28. Merrill Lynch and Age Wave, *Leisure in Retirement: Beyond the Bucket List*
     (Charlotte, NC: Bank of America, 2016), http://agewave.com/wp-content/
     uploads/2016/05/2016-Leisure-in-Retirement_Beyond-the-Bucket-List.pdf

29. Jill Cornfield, "Bankrate Survey."

CONVERSATION 2

1.   Eckhart Tolle, *A New Earth: Awakening to Your Life's Purpose* (New York:
     Penguin, 2005).

2.   Judith E. Glaser, *Conversational Intelligence: How Great Leaders Build Trust and
     Get Extraordinary Results* (London: Routledge, 2016), 16-17.

3.   Wayne W. Dyer, *The Power of Intention: Change the Way You Look at Things and
     the Things You Look at Will Change* (Carlsbad, CA: Hay House, 2001).

CONVERSATION 3

1. Don Steinberg, "Boomer Stars Who Can't Resist a Comeback," *Wall Street Journal*, August 1, 2017, https://www.wsj.com/articles/boomer-stars-who-cant-resist-a-comeback-1501604217

2. Royale Scuderi, "The Best Way to Create a Vision for the Life You Want," https://www.lifehack.org/articles/lifestyle/create-a-vision-for-the-life-you-want.html

3. Royale Scuderi, "The Best Way to Create a Vision for the Life You Want."

4. James O. Prochaska, John C. Norcross, and Carlo C. DiClemente, *Changing for Good: A Revolutionary Six-Stage Program for Overcoming Bad Habits and Moving Your Life Positively Forward* (New York: Harper Collins, 1994).

5. James O. Prochaska et al., *Changing for Good*, 151.

6. James O. Prochaska et al., *Changing for Good*, 156.

CONVERSATION 4

1. Antoine de Saint-Exupéry, *The Little Prince*, trans. Katherine Woods (New York: Harcourt Brace, 1970), 80.

2. *Today Show* [Hoda Kotb interview with Sandra Bullock], NBC, June 4, 2018.

3. Childre, D., Martin, H., Rozman, D., & McCraty, R. *Heart Intelligence, Connecting With the Intuitive Guidance of the Heart,* HeartMath, 2016, p. 7.

4. HeartMath, "Benefits of HeartMath," https://www.heartmath.com/.

5. HeartMath Institute, "HeartMath® Appreciation Tool™ and Exercises," https://www.heartmath.org/resources/heartmath-tools/heartmath-appreciation-tool-and-exercises/

6. HeartMath Institute, "HeartMath® Appreciation Tool™ and Exercises."

7. Stephen Cope, *Soul Friends: The Transforming Power of Deep Human Connection* (Carlsbad, CA: Hay House, 2017).

8. Walter Updegrave, "Ask the Expert" [column], *Money Magazine*, February 17, 2010.

9. Robert Sapolsky, *Behave: The Biology of Humans at Our Best and Worst* (New York: Penguin, 2017).

10. Jim Collins, *Good to Great: Why Some Companies Make the Leap . . . and Others Don't* (New York: HarperCollins, 2011), 41–42.

11.   Robert Dunham, "The Generative Foundations of Action in Organizations: Speaking and Listening," *International Journal of Coaching in Organizations* 7, no. 2 (2009): 48.

12.   Biography.com, "Chesley Sullenberger," https://www.biography.com/people/chesley-sullenberger-20851353

13.   Todd Komarnicki, Chesley Sullenberger, and Jeffrey Zaslow, *Sully* [DVD], directed by Clint Eastwood (Los Angeles: Flashlight Films, 2016).

CONVERSATION 5

1.   Jim Collins, *Good to Great: Why Some Companies Make the Leap . . . and Others Don't* (New York: HarperCollins, 2011), 165.

2.   Peter Block, *The Answer to How Is Yes: Acting on What Matters* (Oakland, CA: Berrett-Koehler, 2003), 10.

3.   Al Switzler, Joseph Grenny, and Ron McMillan, *Crucial Conversations: Tools for Talking When Stakes Are High* (New York: McGraw-Hill Education, 2002).

4.   Robert Dunham, "The Generative Foundations of Action in Organizations: Speaking and Listening," *International Journal of Coaching in Organizations* 7, no. 2 (2009): 43–63.

5.   Robert Dunham, "The Generative Foundations of Action in Organizations."

6.   Maggie Dort, "Ten Days in Whitehorse," in *Transits: Stories From In-Between*, ed. Jaime Forsythe (Picton, Canada: Invisible Publishing, 2007).

7.   J. R. R. Tolkien, "All that is gold does not glitter" [poem], *Lord of the Rings: The Fellowship of the Ring* (London: Allen & Unwin, 1954).

8.   *Oxford English Dictionary*, "Ultimatum," https://en.oxforddictionaries.com/definition/ultimatum

9.   Emily Seppälä, "Connect to Thrive: Social Connection Improves Health, Well-Being & Longevity," *Psychology Today*, August 26, 2012, https://www.psychologytoday.com/blog/feeling-it/201208/connect-thrive

10.   Barry Schwartz, "The Paradox of Choice" [TED Talk], July 2005, https://www.ted.com/talks/barry_schwartz_on_the_paradox_of_choice

11.   Michael Rubin, "Steps to Retirement: How Will You Spend Your Time?" The Balance, June 16, 2018, https://www.thebalance.com/how-you-will-spend-your-retirement-2894357

12.   WebMD, "How to Sleep Better as You Get Older," 2017, https://www.webmd.com/sleep-disorders/guide/aging-affects-sleep#1

13. E. Garcia-Rill, "Reticular Activating System," in *Encyclopedia of Neuroscience*, ed. Larry R. Squire (Cambridge, MA: Academic Press, 2009), 137–143.

14. Dean Bokhari, "The Power of Focusing on What You Want (How Your Brain's Reticular Activating System Functions in Your Favor)," MeaningfulHQ, https://www.meaningfulhq.com/reticular-activating-system-function.html

15. Royale Scuderi, "The Best Way to Create a Vision for the Life You Want," Lifehack, https://www.lifehack.org/articles/lifestyle/create-a-vision-for-the-life-you-want.html

16. Robert Maurer, *One Small Step Can Change Your Life: The Kaizen Way* (New York: Workman, 2004).

17. *Oxford English Dictionary*, "Play," https://en.oxforddictionaries.com/definition/play

CONVERSATION 6

1. University of Kentucky, "But They Did Not Give Up," https://www.uky.edu/~eushe2/Pajares/OnFailingG.html

2. Henry Ford, *My Life and Work* (New York: Doubleday, 1923).

3. Jon Kabat-Zinn, *Wherever You Go, There You Are: Mindfulness Meditation in Everyday Life* (New York: Hyperion, 1994), 4.

4. Gary Gach, *Pause, Breathe, Smile: Awakening Mindfulness When Meditation Is Not Enough* (Louisville, CO: Sounds True, 2018).

5. Eckhart Tolle, *The Power of Now: A Guide to Spiritual Enlightenment* (Vancouver, Canada: Namaste, 1997), 41.

6. Eckhart Tolle, *Stillness Speaks* (Novato, CA: New World Library, 2003), 15.

7. Justin Zackham, *The Bucket List* [DVD], directed by Rob Reiner (Los Angeles: Warner Brothers, 2007).

8. John Coleman, "Lifelong Learning Is Good for Your Health, Your Wallet, and Your Social Life," *Harvard Business Review*, February 7, 2017.

9. Childre, D., Martin, H., Rozman, D., & McCraty, R. *Heart Intelligence, Connecting With the Intuitive Guidance of the Heart*. HeartMath, 2016, pp. 34–37.

CONVERSATION 7

1. *Merriam-Webster Dictionary*, "Self-Fulfillment," https://www.merriam-webster.com/dictionary/self-fulfillment

2. *Oxford English Dictionary*, "Spiritual," https://en.oxforddictionaries.com/definition/spiritual

3. Isabel Allende, "Passion and Aging: Isabel Allende at TED2014" [TED Talk], March 20, 2014, https://blog.ted.com/passion-and-aging-isabel-allende-at-ted2014/

4. Justin Zackham, *The Bucket List* [DVD], directed by Rob Reiner (Los Angeles: Warner Brothers, 2007).

5. Julianne Holt-Lunstad, Timothy B. Smith, and J. Bradley Layton, "Social Relationships and Mortality Risk: A Meta-Analytic Review," *PLOS Medicine* 7, 7 (2010): e1000316.

6. Mark Hyman, "5 Things We Learned From the *Broken Brain* Docuseries," https://drhyman.com/blog/2017/10/27/5-things-learned-broken-brain-docuseries/

7. Leo Widrich, "What Happens to Our Brains When We Exercise and How It Makes Us Happier," February 24, 2014, Fast Company, https://www.fastcompany.com/3025957/what-happens-to-our-brains-when-we-exercise-and-how-it-makes-us-happier

    Mark P. Mattson, "Energy Intake and Exercise as Determinants of Brain Health and Vulnerability to Injury and Disease," *Cell Metabolism* 16 (2012): 706–722.

8. Leo Widrich, "What Happens to Our Brains When We Exercise and How It Makes Us Happier."

9. Davidji, *Secrets of Meditation: A Practical Guide to Inner Peace and Personal Meditation* (Carlsbad, CA: Hay House, 2001).

10. Sarah McKay, "The Neuroscience of Mindfulness Meditation," Chopra Center, https://chopra.com/articles/the-neuroscience-of-mindfulness-meditation?_ga=2.257397768.227223555.1544113604-1694241866.1538868586

11. Deepak Chopra, MD, and Rudolph E. Tanzi, PhD, *Super Genes: Unlock the Astonishing Power of Your DNA for Optimum Health and Well-Being* (New York: Harmony, 2015).

12. Stuart Heller and David Sheppard Surrenda, *Retooling on the Run: Real Change for Leaders With No Time* (Berkeley, CA: North Atlantic, 1995), 33.

13. Stuart Heller and David Sheppard Surrenda, *Retooling on the Run*, 36–37.

14. The Chopra Center, "Top 30 Deepak Chopra Quotes," https://chopra.com/articles/best-deepak-quotes

15. "The Significance of the Asanas and Pranayamas: Language of the Body," Yoga in Daily Life, https://www.yogaindailylife.org/practice-yoga/system-pillars/yoga-pranayama

16. Deepak Chopra, MD, and Rudolph E. Tanzi, PhD, *The Healing Self: A Revolutionary New Plan to Supercharge Your Immunity and Stay Well for Life* (New York: Harmony, 2018), 196–197.

17. Andrew Weil, "4–7–8 Breathing Technique" [video], YouTube, March 22, 2017, https://www.youtube.com/watch?v=_-C_VNM1Vd0

18. Conscious Health, "Benefits of Breathing Exercise: Pranayama," May 25, 2013, http://conscioushealth.net/pranayam-breathing-exercise-conscious-health-nahid-ameen/

19. Tiny Buddha, "The Quote Archive," https://tinybuddha.com/wisdom-quotes/nothing-grateful-check-pulse/

20. Nick Ortner, "Incredible Research That Will Make You Instantly Healthier," The Tapping Solution, https://www.thetappingsolution.com/science-research/

21. Nick Ortner, *The Tapping Solution: A Revolutionary System for Stress-Free Living* (Carlsbad, CA: Hay House, 2013).

22. Shamans Market, "The Power of *Despacho* Ceremonies" [blog], September 20, 2017, http://blog.shamansmarket.com/power-despacho-ceremonies/

23. Shamans Market, "The Power of *Despacho* Ceremonies."

24. Daring to Live Fully, "Harvard's Most Popular Course: Tal Ben-Shahar on How to Be Happy," https://daringtolivefully.com/happier-tal-ben-shahar

25. Yagana Shah, "New Study Proves That Laughter Really Is the Best Medicine," *Huffington Post*, April 22, 2014, https://www.huffingtonpost.com/2014/04/22/laughter-and-memory_n_5192086.html

26. Yagana Shah, "New Study Proves That Laughter Really Is the Best Medicine."

27. Clinton Colmenares, "No Joke: Study Finds Laughing Can Burn Calories," *Reporter*, June 10, 2005, http://www.mc.vanderbilt.edu/reporter/index.html?ID=4030

28. University of Maryland Medical Center, "Laughter Is Good for Your Heart, According to a New University of Maryland Medical Center Study," *Science Daily*, November 17, 2000, https://www.sciencedaily.com/releases/2000/11/001116080726.htm

29. Peter Kelder, *Ancient Secret of the Fountain of Youth* (New York: Doubleday, 1998).

30. Dawson Church, *The Genie in Your Genes: Epigenetic Medicine and the New Biology of Intention* (Santa Rosa, CA: Energy Psychology Press, 2007).

31. Eckhart Tolle, *A New Earth: Awakening to Your Life's Purpose* (New York: Penguin, 2006), 166.

32. Isabel Allende, *Island Beneath the Sea* (New York: Harper, 2010), 319.

33. John B. Izzo, *Second Innocence: Rediscovering Joy and Wonder: A Guide to Renewal in Work, Relationships, and Daily Life* (Oakland, CA: Berrett-Koehler, 2004).

34. John Izzo, *Second Innocence*, 1.

35. Angeles Arrien, *The Second Half of Life: Opening the Eight Gates of Wisdom* (Louisville, CO: Sounds True, 1998).

36. Mary Corrigan, "When It's Over, It's Over" [blog], Creativity for the Rest of Us With Marry Corrigan, June 18, 2012, http://www.creativity4us.com/gratitude/when-its-over-its-over/

37. Mary Corrigan, "When It's Over, It's Over."

LAGNIAPPE

1. Patrick O'Neill, *The Only Certain Freedom: The Transformative Journey of the Entrepreneur* (self-published, 2018).

2. Patrick O'Neill, "Your Vitality" [blog], Extraordinary Conversations, July 23, 2013, http://extraordinaryconversations.com/thought-leadership/2013/5/23/your-vitality

3. Patrick O'Neill, "Your Vitality."

4. Grandma Moses, *My Life's History* (New York: Harper, 1952).

5. Renee Stepler, "World's Centenarian Population Projected to Grown Eightfold by 2050," Pew Research Center, April 21, 2016, http://www.pewresearch.org/fact-tank/2016/04/21/worlds-centenarian-population-projected-to-grow-eightfold-by-2050/

6. Associated Press, "Centenarians Are the Fastest-Growing Age Segment: Number of 100-Year-Olds to Hit 6 Million by 2050," *New York Daily News*, July 21, 2009, http://www.nydailynews.com/life-style/centenarians-fastest-growing-age-segment-number-100-year-olds-hit-6-million-2050-article-1.400828

7. Dan Buettner, "Power 9®: Reverse Engineering Longevity," Blue Zones Project, https://www.bluezones.com/2016/11/power-9/

8. Alex Riley, "The Secret to a Long and Healthy Life? Eat Less," BBC, June 1, 2017, http://www.bbc.com/future/story/20170601-the-secret-to-a-long-and-healthy-life-eat-less

9. Julie A. Mattison et al., "Caloric Restriction Improves Health and Survival of Rhesus Monkeys," *Nature Communications* 8 (2017): Article 14063.

10. Dan Buettner, "Power 9°."

11. Dan Buettner, "Power 9°."

12. "Fort Worth Blue Zone Shines," *Natural Awakenings*, May 2018, https://www.nadallas.com/DAL/May-2018/Fort-Worth-Blue-Zone-Shines/

13. "Future of Healthcare Is Creating Environmental Change," Blue Zones Project, https://www.bluezones.com/2018/08/future-of-health-care-is-creating-environmental-change/

   "Blue Zones Project Case Study: Albert Lea, MN," Blue Zones Project, March 26, 2017, http://bluezonesproject.hs-sites.com/albertlea/blue-zones-project-case-study-albert-lea-mn

14. Medical Research Council Mitochondrial Biology Unit, "What Are Mitochondria?" http://www.mrc-mbu.cam.ac.uk/what-are-mitochondria

15. Pamela Weintraub, "The Care and Feeding of Your Mitochondria," Experience Life, November 2014, https://experiencelife.com/article/the-care-and-feeding-of-your-mitochondria/

16. Human Longevity Project, *The Human Longevity Project: A Blueprint for Health and Longevity in the Modern World*, https://humanlongevityfilm.com/downloads/transcripts/thlp_actionplan_1.pdf

   Pamela Weintraub, "The Care and Feeding of Your Mitochondria."

17. Mark Hyman, "About Functional Medicine," http://drhyman.com/about-2/about-functional-medicine/

18. Mark Hyman, *The UltraMind Solution: Fix Your Broken Brain by Healing Your Body First* (New York: Scribner, 2008).

19. Christiane Northrup, *Goddesses Never Age: The Secret Prescription for Radiance, Vitality and Well-Being* (Carlsbad, CA: Hay House, 2015).

20. Arianna Huffington, *Thrive: The Third Metric to Redefining Success and Creating a Life of Well-Being, Wisdom, and Wonder* (New York: Harmony, 2014).

21. Arianna Huffington, *Thrive*, 75.

22. Arianna Huffington, *Thrive*, 62.

23. Bessie A. Stanley. Essay. *Emporia Gazette*, December 11, 1905.

APPENDIX C

1. Anodea Judith, *Anodea Judith's Chakra Yoga* (Woodbury, MN: Llewellyn, 2015).

2. Anodea Judith, "Anodea Judith's Chakra Yoga" [interview], retrieved from http://anodeajudith.com/anodea-judiths-chakra-yoga/

3. Anodea Judith and Lion Goodman, *Creating on Purpose: The Spiritual Technology of Manifesting Through the Chakras* (Boulder, CO: Sounds True, 2012).

ACKNOWLEDGEMENTS

Where do we begin?

First, we want to thank Valerie Fulbright for that memorable dinner conversation shared in the Introduction. She sparked our commitment to writing a book about Retirement Rebels who are living their Next Chapter with talent, energy, and a desire to continue making a difference.

Next, our gratitude extends to all the people who allowed us to share their experiences and stories throughout this book. Through their rich, unique, and often unexpected perspectives, they added layers of depth to the book's messages.

Listed in the order of where their stories appear in the book, our contributors include: Ellie Aronoff, Linda Brady, Wayne Caskey, Margie Herring, Carolyn Carson, Anita, Bev & Ray Mentzer, Cathy Helmbrecht, Debbie Taylor, Ann Saegert, Deb and Don Teeples, Eric Anderson, Bill Helmbrecht, Pat Bonds, Charley Kienzle, Mike Sharry, Shirley Anderson, Mary Ellen & Bill England, Noel Hensley, Cheryl Cummings, Phil Davis, Sheri Lewis, Graceanna Jones, Chet Curtis, Tom Degnan Jr., Margaret Skaggs, Bob Salerno, Bev Goulet, Ruthy Friedman, Ronald C. Parker, Mary Sue Seibold, Barry McPherson, Jan Sharry, Linda Catt, Sheryl Wylie, Becky Frank, Darlene Elkins, Tom Ervolina, Karren McClure, Terri West, David Cummings, Karen Stuart, Caroline Kienzle, Leita Hamill, Margery

Miller, Sue Romanowski, Rich Fedock, Curt FitzGerald, Ed Galante, Kathy Burke, Suzanne (Max) Maxwell, Debbie Townsend, Ann Bentley, Bob Dunham, and John Lazar. Once again, many thanks to all of you!

We also thank our dear friends with whom we have conversations, travel, laugh, and play. Each one of them contributed directly or indirectly to this book.

Our thanks also extend to all our clients and professional colleagues. Through working with them, we have learned about leadership greatness and the many ways it can be demonstrated.

While writing this book, we incorporated the teachings and research of many writers, experts, and scholars. We have made our best effort to acknowledge their work properly and provide correct references so that others can have easy access to their wisdom.

A special expression of appreciation goes to our editors, book advisors, and work associates who have been by our sides during the creation of *Retirement Your Way*—our first book. Without each one of them, this book would still be in process. Thanks to Suzanne Bellavista Murray, Rachel Fending, Jerry Dorris, Vickie Sullivan, Terry Stevens, Valerie Bonds, Sue Romanowski, and all the talented coaches at Quantum Leap.

We also would like to thank all of our personal role models, mentors, and teachers along the way who have given us knowledge, insights, advice, and a joy for experimentation. Thanks and love from Marilyn go to her sister Peggy Foster and her brother Ray Longino who are, and always will be, her role models – and to Noah Blumenthal and Mike Jaffe for their support and encouragement to us in this process. Gail remembers and thanks her earliest role models and advisors from her days as a student— Juanita Kreps, Marion Kellogg, and Ned Rosen—who showed her what she could be and do in the world.

Most importantly, we extend our love and gratitude to our families. Our parents and grandparents have passed on, yet they are our inspiration from the past. In particular, we thank our incredible parents, Gladys and Macey Longino and Hazel and Jim McDonald for loving and inspiring us. We hold them in our hearts, and we remember how they lived with honor, resourcefulness, and contribution throughout their lives. They are our role models for a joyful Next Chapter.

Our love and gratitude also extend to our immediate families who are our inspiration for the present and the future. Our husbands, Jeff and Brian, read our manuscript multiple times, helped us to fine-tune many of the points, and provided continual support during the ups and downs. They were—and continue to be—our lifelines.

As we look to the generations that follow us, Marilyn's niece Melanie and nephew Les bring ongoing joy and happiness into her life, and she feels the daily presence of her niece Mindy and nephew Carlo who live on in her heart. Gail's daughters, Lindsey and Jaime, sons-in-law, Nick and JR, and four grandchildren—Logan, Amelia, Taylor, and Will—touch her heart deeply and provide uncountable moments of joy! Life is much brighter when they are around!

Gail M. McDonald

Gail McDonald is President of Transition Resources, Inc., where she specializes in executive coaching, team coaching, and meeting facilitation. Her clients span multiple industries, including high-tech, banking, financial services, aerospace, manufacturing, transportation, distribution, and nonprofit.

Prior to forming her own company, Gail worked in four corporations, including Ryder System, Inc. where she served as a C-level executive. She is a member of the Board of Directors for the United Way of Metropolitan Dallas (UWMD) and for the Children's Medical Center Foundation of Dallas. She holds several certifications, including Professional Certified Coach (PCC) from the International Coach Federation.

Gail and her husband, Jeff Murphy, live in Dallas, Texas where they spend their free time traveling, playing bridge, and enjoying their family, including their daughters and sons-in-law, Lindsey, Jaime, Nick, and JR, plus their four incredible grandchildren.

Marilyn L. Bushey

Marilyn Bushey is the CEO of PowerPAC, Inc., and is an executive coach, facilitator, and leadership consultant. Her clients include leaders in the banking, distribution, healthcare, manufacturing, insurance, government, high-tech, financial services, colleges and nonprofits.

Marilyn is a serial entrepreneur and has owned or been an owner in three businesses. She is a former national board member of the National Association of Women Business Owners (NAWBO) and was awarded the first Lifetime Achievement Award given by the organization. She was also recognized by City of Irving as a High Spirited Citizen for her outstanding contributions to the Irving Community.

Marilyn enjoys a busy social life and is an avid reader and movie buff. She lives in Texas, on the banks of Lake Lewisville with her husband Brian and their cat Golden.

FOR MORE INFORMATION

For more information about our programs and services, please visit our website (www.retirementyourwaybook.com) to see our latest offerings or our Facebook page (Retirement Your Way) to join the conversation.

Made in the USA
Monee, IL
10 October 2023